T0023347

# A YEAR
## IN THE LIFE OF
# ANCIENT
# EGYPT

Also by Donald P. Ryan

*24 Hours in Ancient Egypt*

# A YEAR
# IN THE LIFE OF
# ANCIENT
# EGYPT

## THE REAL LIVES OF THE
## PEOPLE WHO LIVED THERE

### DONALD P. RYAN

Michael O'Mara Books Limited

First published in Great Britain in 2022 by
Michael O'Mara Books Limited
9 Lion Yard
Tremadoc Road
London SW4 7NQ

A CIP catalogue record for this book is available from the British
Library.

Papers used by Michael O'Mara Books Limited are natural,
recyclable products made from wood grown in sustainable
forests. The manufacturing processes conform to the
environmental regulations of the country of origin.

ISBN: 978-1-78929-365-4 in hardback print format
ISBN: 978-1-78929-366-1 in ebook format

1 2 3 4 5 6 7 8 9 10

Designed and typeset by Ed Pickford
Printed and bound by CPI Group (UK) Ltd, Croydon, CR0 4YY

www.mombooks.com

*In memory of*

*Dorothy Aubinoe Shelton, Patricia Chant Armstrong Ryan,*

*Shirley Amdam McKean and Kim Nesselquist*

# Contents

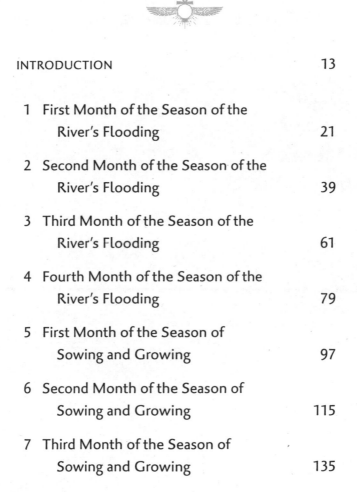

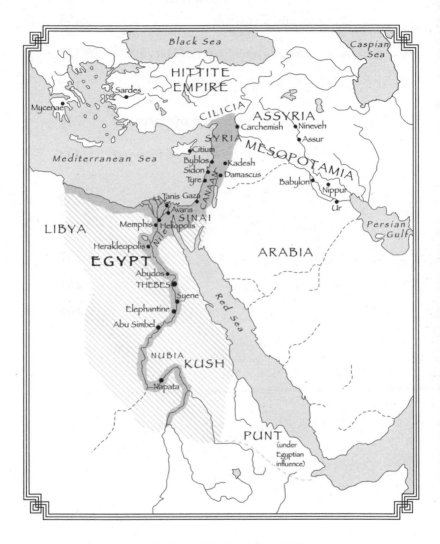

THE EGYPTIAN EMPIRE
15TH CENTURY BC

# Egyptian Chronology

| | |
|---|---|
| Early Dynastic Period | *c.* 3000–2686 BC |
| Old Kingdom | 2686–2125 BC |
| First Intermediate Period | 2160–2055 BC |
| Middle Kingdom | 2055–1650 BC |
| Second Intermediate Period | 1650–1550 BC |
| New Kingdom | 1550–1069 BC |
| Third Intermediate Period | 1069–664 BC |
| Late Period | 664–332 BC |
| Graeco-Roman Period | 332 BC – AD 395 |

# Introduction

When it comes to ancient cultures, Egypt seems to maintain an irrepressible allure. In our modern era, we continue to be amazed, puzzled and delighted by that civilization, which flourished for around three thousand years but left us only with sundry and often curious traces to reconstruct its former glory. This book presents a glimpse of that land over the course of twelve months during which we can view the lives of several of its inhabitants, from the ordinary to the royal. The point in time is the twenty-sixth year of the reign of the pharaoh Amenhotep II (*c.* 1400 BC).

In our story we'll meet not only Amenhotep II and his family, but several of his numerous underlings who comprised the vast Egyptian bureaucracy of administrators, soldiers and priests. While rulers, officials and other elites have left us with some tangible evidence of their deeds, it should never be forgotten that the great achievements of the ancient Egyptians were based on a foundation of ordinary people, including farmers, fishermen, potters, artisans, brick-makers and brewers, who lived in a beautiful land they believed to be overseen by supernatural forces.

The ancient Egyptian civilization seems to have been established by about 3050 BC, if one defines 'civilization' as a culture with characteristics of what anthropologists refer to as a 'complex society'. These traits often include a ruler supported by a hierarchy of officials, differences in wealth amongst the population, craft specialists, the building of monuments (typically palaces and temples) and a system of writing. The ancient Egyptians themselves claimed that their civilization began with the political unification of the two parts of their great land: Upper Egypt, comprising the Nile Valley in the south, and Lower Egypt, encompassing the Nile Delta in the north.

Based on ancient sources, Egyptian history has traditionally been divided into thirty dynasties, ideally groups of related rulers, arranged into named 'periods' and three 'kingdoms', which allow us to place specific individuals and events in time. The eras known as 'kingdoms' were times when Egypt was unified, prosperous and at its most sophisticated, when many of the great monuments familiar to most of us were built. The 'intermediate' and other 'periods' were times of instability and/or episodes of foreign rule.

The Old Kingdom (c. 2686–2125 BC) is best known as the era when the great stone pyramids were constructed. The Middle Kingdom (c. 2055–1650 BC) is considered a classical age when literature and the arts flourished, and the New Kingdom (c. 1550–1069 BC) is the age of empire during which Egypt expanded its control well beyond its borders in areas to the south and east. The period in which this book is set is during the first of the three dynasties of the New Kingdom – the 18th overall – and it was a remarkable time indeed. Here we find some incredible rulers including warrior pharaohs, a female pharaoh, a royal religious heretic, and the so-called 'boy-king' Tutankhamun, during a time of great wealth. In the three thousand years of Egyptian civilization, the 18th dynasty began around the middle of that span, c. 1550 BC, about a thousand years after the famed Great Pyramid at Giza was constructed, and over a thousand years before the reign of the oft-romanticized Greek ruler Cleopatra.

The ancient Egyptians organized their lives on the basis of a calendar that wasn't too much different from that which most people use today. They had an annual civil calendar consisting of twelve months of thirty days each, with each day divided into twenty-four hours. There were three seasons of four months, plus an additional five days to approximately match the 365 day natural cycle. The three seasons were that of the flooding of the Nile (approximately mid-July to about mid-November), the season of sowing and growing (mid-November to mid-March) and the time of harvest (mid-March to mid-July). Similar to modern times, the months equivalent to our autumn and winter were quite pleasant during the day and perhaps a bit chilly during the evening. The heat would begin to pick up in the spring with the summer months quite hot.

Certain annual events, such as festivals, were assigned to specific days or cycles of the moon during a particular season and month. In terms of identifying specific events, dates could be indicated based on the reign of an individual pharaoh, for example: Year 15, Month 3 of the

Season of Sowing and Growing, Day 5 under the majesty of Thutmose III.

Several of the individuals in this book are historically attested characters including Amenhotep II, of course, and his family, including his successor Thutmose IV, along with several of his officials who are fairly well known from surviving monuments. The fact remains, however, that we know few details of the lives of the majority of ordinary individuals upon which the ancient Egyptian civilization was sustained. While pharaohs boasted of their achievements on temple walls and through impressive stone statuary, and wealthy officials made themselves known with their own statues and painted tombs, the average farmers and craftsmen were illiterate and went about their lives unsung, but still utterly vital in society.

Much of what we know about that culture comes from the remains of temples and tombs, monuments of religion and death built to endure for eternity but representing just a slice of life, and much of it coming from the south of Egypt, where environmental conditions are more favourable to the survival of archaeological remains through the ages. Living in mud-brick houses on the banks of the annually flooding Nile isn't particularly conducive to the long-term survival of the homes and villages where most Egyptians lived. Fortunately, a few unique communities have survived to inform us of some of the details, one being the village that housed the workmen who built the royal tombs during the New Kingdom, and a couple of others that facilitated those who built the pyramids during earlier ages, all situated sufficiently safe from the inundations. In short, our knowledge of ancient Egyptian life is somewhat uneven and unrepresentative of all of society.

As ancient Egypt was a culture with writing for the relatively few trained in its use, scholars have been blessed with a good number of inscriptions and other documents that have provided us with precious insights into many aspects of ancient life. Our ability now to read the hieroglyphs and other Egyptian scripts with some degree of accuracy has provided us with some information about historical, economic, religious and personal matters, and also gives us a peek into the ancient mind and ways of thinking. Egyptologists also have benefited from some of the observations of ancient foreign visitors, notably Greeks and Romans, who wrote about their experiences in Egypt, although many centuries after the time described in this book.

Much of the action in our year-long story takes place in two of Egypt's major cities, the ancient capital of Memphis, near modern-day Cairo, and Thebes, much further south, a city of profound religious importance and home to a number of immense temples. If we visit the site of Memphis today, it survives as acres of collapsed mud-brick walls leaving one straining to imagine its former glory. As for Thebes, many of its temples endure, although deteriorating, but in its adjacent cemeteries are numerous tombs of officials, their walls painted with idealized scenes of daily life, thus providing us with unique, interpretable insights. Given the bias in the survival of temples and tombs, we shouldn't gain the impression that the Egyptians were obsessed with religion and death. It does seem that they took the relationships with their gods seriously, but not to the point that it was a preoccupation for most. As for death, it's clear that the Egyptians were more obsessed with life, and hoped to be spiritually resurrected into a pain-free version of the beautiful land they loved.

Despite the piecemeal evidence from here and there, archaeologists and Egyptologists have been able to gain a reasonable grasp of what it was like to live in ancient Egypt, although we can never be sure that our ideas are fully accurate or complete. Regardless, this book will paint a diverse picture of a particular year – and an interesting year at that – by presenting stories representing a cross-section of ancient Egyptian society and some of the people who lived in that remarkable place and time. And despite the modern fascination with pyramids, mummies, tombs and gold that has left many with mysterious ideas of the ancient Egyptians, you will find them to be very human, experiencing similar drudgery, joy and sorrows in their lives millennia ago just as we do now.

The reader should understand that the purpose of this book is to give an impression of ancient Egypt at a time when it was flourishing. It is a kind of historical fiction, that is, borrowing from what we know and incorporating it into story-telling. As noted, the majority of ancient Egyptians were illiterate and their voices mostly muted apart from what others wrote about them, depictions of daily life on tomb walls, or from the interpretation of archaeological materials. Although we do know more about the rulers and the elite than the millions who supported them, our information is nowhere complete. It should be understood that even their stories, too, can be somewhat speculative. For example, although there is very suggestive evidence that there was some sort of controversy regarding the succession of Thutmose IV, in this book I present my own scenario, which, though plausible, can't be confirmed given the scarcity of evidence. And we can only guess at the cause of death of his father, Amenhotep II, as an examination of his mummy has thus far not revealed a specific reason.

Another Egyptologist writing this book would no doubt create different characters and situations to describe a year in the life of ancient Egypt. But in this volume, you'll read my own version coloured by my personal knowledge and experience in the subject. I hope you, the reader, will find it informative, interesting and regularly entertaining.

# First Month of the Season
of the River's Flooding

## THE FARMER

The blackness of a moonless night gave way to fading stars, and a slight and then growing tinge of grey. Alerted by the subtly growing light, a dozen species of birds contributed their voices to the anticipated grand phenomenon about to take place. As the grey gradually turned to a faint pink, the outlines of the surroundings gradually became visible: palms, acacias and the dark forms of mountains in the distance.

Baki lay on his side, awakening without prompt at an early hour as one who tends fields is accustomed. With a groan, he rolled over on his woven mat and accepted the fact that his sleep was over, at least for the moment. His two children were still curled up on the other side of the room but his wife, Mutui, had predictably arisen well before and her voice could be heard outside, softly singing as she began her usual daily chores. Grabbing a woven basket, she snatched handfuls of grain from the home's ample granary, and knelt down before a polished rock slab. The rhythmic pounding and scraping of a smooth stone transforming wheat into flour was almost as comforting as the daily rising of the sun itself, bringing light and warmth every day, or at least one hopes it will continue to appear each morning.

With bleary eyes blinking in nervous anticipation, Baki arose to witness the unfolding celestial drama as he took his place on a brick bench in front of his simple home. Soon, he fervently prayed, a brilliant, glowing, warming orb would appear in full glory on the horizon, and begin its daily traverse of the sky. It was not to be taken for granted. Although Baki had rarely experienced a day that wasn't at least partially sunny, he was well aware that if sufficient petition, appeasement and adoration weren't consistently offered, the land he loved and thrived upon could be sunk into cold, darkness and death. Baki didn't wait long, and he sighed with relief as the edge of the blazing glowing orb that is the god Re appeared on the horizon. Re, after disappearing into the west twelve hours previously, had died but had yet again successfully survived a night of defeating obstacles and perils in the Netherworld, to reappear triumphantly announcing a new day.

Re had never done otherwise, but that was only because he was sufficiently satisfied, at least in part by a large network of priests officiating in grandiose temples, ultimately presided over by the highest priest of all,

Aakheperure Amenhotep, the ruler of the entire land. The priests must be doing their job well, surmised Baki. The sun god in his various forms continues to be appeased.

Re could be perceived in many variations. He could be seen as Re-Harakhty in the form of a great cosmic hawk whose wings slowly propelled the fiery disc across the daytime sky. Or one could view its propulsion as the result of a massive scarab beetle in the sky, who like the terrestrial version, which rolls a ball of egg-bearing dung before itself, pushes the great orange sphere towards the west. Or was it a great ship, plying the heavens with a contingency of gods aboard? And there was the Aten with its life-nurturing rays; but perhaps the strongest manifestation of all was Amun-Re, the sun embodied with the triumphant national god, the mighty yet unseen Amun.

SOME OF THE EGYPTIAN DEITIES NOTED IN THIS BOOK (FROM LEFT TO RIGHT): AMUN-RE, OSIRIS AND ISIS, HATHOR AND BES

Amun was certainly overwhelmingly powerful these days. His temples were imposing, prolific and wealthy and his priests were numerous. Even the ruler's name, Amenhotep – 'Amun is satisfied' – was a regular reminder of his greatness. Although Re and Amun were supreme, there were hundreds of other gods and goddesses, spirits and demons, who needed to be recognized and appeased or occasionally vanquished, representing all conceivable aspects of life and death. There was, for example, the goddess Hathor, who in the form of a cow could be a nurturing mother, but in the form of Sekhmet could be a fierce, bloodthirsty and protective lioness. On the kinder and more abstract spectrum was Thoth, who could be perceived as an ibis bird, and sometimes a baboon, and represented wisdom and writing.

There was Seth, who represented chaos, and Maat who represented stability. And then there were plenty of entities to be found in the life beyond, including Osiris, who ruled the Netherworld, a realm full of tricksters and malevolent creatures, and who presided over the judgement of the deceased. The sun god, Re, had to contend with the great snake, Apophis, who attempted to kill him every night. The gods could variably be depicted in human form, or as an associated animal, or with a human body and appropriate head. If one couldn't read hieroglyphs, the head adornment on the statue or painting could help distinguish one from the other if they appeared similar.

Baki was a farmer, and despite the unrelenting woes of hard physical work, he genuinely loved his land. Gazing across a vast landscape of just-harvested fields,

## THE NAMES OF EGYPT

The name 'Egypt' in English today seems to have its origins in the name of the temple of the god Ptah at Memphis, 'Hut-ka-Ptah' (House of the spirit of Ptah), which became *Aigyptos* in Greek, *Aegyptus* in Latin, *L'Égypte* in French, *Ägypten* in German, etc. In the modern country of Egypt today, the name in Arabic is Masr, its old origins suggesting a fortress or border. After the Greeks colonized Egypt beginning in the fourth century BC, many Egyptian towns acquired Greek names. 'Waset', for example, became 'Thebes', and 'Men-nefer' became 'Memphis'. With the introduction of Arab culture in the seventh century AD, some sites also acquired new place names and ancient Waset/Thebes is today known as 'Luxor'.

he was filled with deep appreciation of its beauty and abundance of produce. The fields lay along the banks of a magnificent river that wound its way from south to north to empty into the Great Green, a sea that Baki had only heard of (the Mediterranean). Believing that the flat earth was surrounded by waters above and waters below, ancient Egyptians imagined that the Nile percolated from a source below, somewhere far to the south.

The river itself, the Nile, was a great wonder. In a normal year, its waters would rise and recede over a period of a few months, leaving the fields renewed with a rich black fertile muck that was perfect for growing essential crops such as wheat, barley and flax. As a result of this annual flooding and its fruitful outcome, Baki and his people called the land *Kemet* – the Black Land – referring to the rich fertility of the soil that allowed its people to flourish.

On very rare occasions, the river could flood too much and threaten villages situated on slightly higher ground, or perhaps worse, not rise much at all and cause famine. The great storehouses of surplus grain found throughout the land were a testament to the latter nagging possibility. The

## THE NILE RIVER

The ancient Egyptians referred to the Nile only as 'the river'; it was the only river most knew. With its origins in the lakes of central Africa and the highlands of Ethiopia, it is the longest river in the world at over four thousand miles in length. The name 'Nile' has its origins in the Greek *Neilos*, meaning river valley. Several ancient civilizations, including Mesopotamia and Egypt, developed from agricultural societies established on the banks of rivers. In the case of Egypt, the Nile's annual flood cycle which renewed the soil along its banks, provided an ideal environment for the Egyptian civilization to develop and flourish for millennia.

god Hapi, looking like a well-fed fellow with papyrus plants growing out of his head, represented the annual flood, and would hopefully remain more content than otherwise.

The river's beneficial qualities weren't confined to renewing the fields; its waters were teeming with many kinds of fish, and its shores were abundant with edible fowl and useful plants. It also served as a natural highway with its waters coursing north but its prevailing winds blowing south to fill the sails of those travelling in that direction. On most days, the river was alive with activity, with fishermen and others working along its banks, and ships of all sizes travelling in both directions.

Off to the east lay generally inhospitable deserts and mountains – the Red Land – and likewise to the west were wide expanses of unwelcoming territory, nearly waterless but spotted with a few oases. Exquisite stone and gold, however, could be quarried and mined in the east, and routes across this dry environ could take one to a great sea (the Red Sea) where maritime expeditions could be launched to exotic lands to the south. Not surprisingly, the vast majority of Kemet/Egypt's millions of people lived directly along the river's shores or on land between its tributaries, there being hundreds of villages and several large population centres.

Like most Egyptians, Baki couldn't read, but had been taught by his elders who shared a general understanding of how his world had come about. There was once a time when there was nothing, but out of this void a god appeared, Atum, emerging from a primeval mound of slime, not unlike those that appeared on the fields as the waters of the annual flooding receded. Atum created a pair of gods, Shu and Tefnut, air and moisture, who in turn produced Nut and Geb, sky and land, all essential for the structure of the world and the maintenance of life. Four other gods were generated that were more human in nature: Osiris and his sister/wife Isis, along with Seth and Nephthys. (And there would be plenty of drama between them!) One of the gods, Khnum, would create humans and their spirits on a potter's wheel and people would live and prosper along the river. Although all of this took place eons ago, the gods were very much still active, and of foremost importance in the continuation of society was the god Horus, the son of Osiris and Isis, who was embodied in the living ruler of Egypt.

Baki had also learned that long ago, there had been disputes between the people of the north – 'Lower Egypt' according to the downstream flow of the Nile, a place where the river splits into several multiple streams of the Nile Delta – and 'Upper Egypt', the relatively narrow and sinuous Nile Valley. More than a thousand years previously, a king of Upper Egypt remembered by the name Menes was successful in uniting the two regions and thereafter, the ruler of Egypt would be known as 'Lord of the Two Lands'.

The capital – most commonly noted today by its Greek name, 'Memphis' – would be strategically established near the juncture of the two, both as an administrative centre for the vast bureaucracy that would emerge, and as a home for the ruler. Dozens of kings had ruled successfully over many centuries, and although Egypt had suffered at least

## EGYPTIAN NATIONALITY

Egypt's xenophobic attitude was based not on race or skin-colour but on ethnicity. Unlike many cultures in the Near Eastern region, Egyptian civilization developed relatively isolated from others due to its geographical situation. Deserts to the east, west and south, and the Mediterranean Sea to the north provided natural boundaries and protection. Unpleasant and sometimes violent encounters with outsiders encouraged the Egyptians' suspicions of foreigners. Outsiders could, however, become Egyptian, provided they fully adapted to, and participated in, Egyptian culture including its language, religion and authority.

two periods of disunity, it always recovered stronger in the aftermath. Egypt had now become so strong that it had reached far beyond its natural borders and controlled foreign lands to both the south and the east that could supply the homeland with great wealth.

Yes, Baki concluded, it was better to be an Egyptian than anything else. All who were not, he was taught, were inferior. To the south, beyond Egypt's southern borders, were the typically uncooperative and surly inhabitants of Kush (Nubia). They had to be dealt with as their land was an irresistible source of exotic products including gold and other precious metals, as well as gems, gorgeous hardwoods, and even strange and curious animals. 'Evil' or 'wretched' were the terms often applied to Kush, and Egypt's rulers took pride in subjugating them to build the wealth of Kemet.

Far to the east and north-east lived numerous people who were likewise considered lowly, and inhabited various towns and cities ripe for conquest. Military adventures in such places as Canaan and Syria were providing tremendous valuable resources including cheap labour by captives who could be assigned some of the most obnoxious of chores. And then, to the north-west, there were the Libyans, whose ways were similarly detestable.

Baki indeed felt lucky. He and his family lived in a village adjacent to the great city of Thebes, a religious capital in the south of Egypt and home to the ruler when he wasn't in his palace in Memphis, or off visiting his realm. There seemed to be always something going on with boats coming and going, a plethora of goods being loaded and unloaded at the city's ports, the comings and goings of Egyptian and foreign officials, and there were incredible temples to the gods, including Amun, the patron of Thebes and, realistically, all of Egypt. Amun's temples in Thebes were almost beyond belief. It was impossible not to be awed by their stunning walls and statuary, and the soaring gold-gilded obelisks exploding with light when struck by the sun's rays.

On the west side of the river, the impressive memorial temples of several previous rulers could be seen from the opposite shore, sacred places where priests assigned to the task still provided regular offerings. And speckling the nearby hills behind were a growing number of elaborate private tombs belonging to Egypt's elite. Beyond lay a not-so-secret secret: a valley that served as a royal cemetery for Egypt's rulers, the once-living god-kings who had shed their mortal responsibilities to spend a divine eternity elsewhere. It might be expected; after all, the west was the land of the dead, where Re descended, and jackals roamed the nocturnal landscape.

## EGYPT'S PROVINCES

Egypt was traditionally divided into forty-two provinces, or *nomes* to use the Greek term commonly applied by modern scholars. Twenty were situated in the north, 'Lower Egypt', with the other twenty-two in southern 'Upper Egypt'. Each had its own name, patron god, and accompanying temple, and was overseen by a governor (*nomarch*) who ultimately answered to the pharaoh and his administration. Egypt's capital, Memphis, was within the first nome of Lower Egypt, the 'White Walls', with its primary god being Ptah. The vitally important city of Thebes was known as the Sceptre nome, where the god Amun reigned supreme. During times of political uncertainty in ancient Egyptian history, some of these nomarchs competed for power with varying results.

Baki returned to his bed and lay on his back, as the new light of day continued to fill the room. It seemed that every bone in his body ached from the previous days' heavy efforts of harvesting what was left of the grain before the river would begin its slow rise and cover the fields. This day was, in fact, the beginning of a new year, the first day of the first of three seasons, and something worthy of celebration. For the moment, at least, Baki was content and looking forward to lighter chores and a bit of rest until the river would expectedly subside in a few months. Then the planting and harvesting would begin anew.

## The New Year's Festival

After but a few minutes of restless sleep, Baki was awakened by the stirring of his giggling children. Mutui had informed them that, yes, this was Wep-Renpet, the annual New Year's Festival, an occasion full of food and frivolity that would last several days. There would be games in the street, an abundance of food, drinks and music, and a few smiles on otherwise stoic faces. It was by no means the only festival during the year, but for many it was the best.

After a small, simple meal of bread and porridge, Baki opened a small chest made of dried and plaited rushes. From within he removed several folded items including simple tube-like dresses for his wife and daughter, and clean white linen skirts for himself and his son. As his family changed into their best outfits for the occasion, Baki reached into the bottom of the chest and removed a prized pair of sandals, which he saved just for special days. Taking the children by the hand, Baki and Mutui walked out into the dusty street to stroll slowly from one end of the village to the other.

With the prestigious city of Thebes being but an hour's walk away, the village had grown substantially as Egypt's wealth increased. Its generally safe position above the usual flood waters was partially due to it having been built atop the ruins of previous settlements, thus creating a substantial raised area that supported hundreds of homes. It was clear that, unlike the formal buildings found in nearby Thebes and elsewhere, there had been very little planning in this community. Each of the small, closely spaced houses seemed at a slightly different angle, and numerous repairs and improvements to their mud-brick walls were evident. Although no two looked the same, most consisted of a few small rooms, and a little open area for a kiln or storage, or even perhaps a donkey. Some had doorways made of scraps of joined wood while others maintained privacy with a hanging mat or sheet. Despite their simplicity, the village homes were actually quite comfortable, their mud-brick walls keeping their interiors cool during the hotter months and relatively warm during the colder. And their flat roofs of mud-plastered palm branches and trunks added to the insulation.

Even mid-morning, the streets were already becoming festive, with fresh foods being sold and shared in front of many of the houses, and an impromptu market forming in a vacant space between a few broken-down shacks.

Children chased each other in the streets and the smell of freshly baked bread sweetened with honey filled the air. Later, there would be splurging on beef and geese, typically the purview of the wealthy, but something that could make any occasion extra-special. And there would be beer – lots of beer – a little more potent than that consumed on an ordinary day, and if lucky, one might get a few sips of local wine.

Having grown up in the village, Baki knew virtually everyone, and most of their personal affairs as well. Very little could be kept private in such close quarters. Births and deaths were known to all almost immediately, and it was difficult to keep romances – both legitimate and otherwise – quiet for very long. Rumours, too, could fly about with varying degrees of truth, but were usually eagerly consumed. Like a large extended family, there were close friends, and long-term feuds.

Walking slowly along the avenue, Baki and Mutui were greeted by most, some of whom had not taken a break from their labours for many weeks. Like Baki, most of the farmers had just finished their tasks and grudgingly paid their taxes. Looking forward to a lighter schedule, they were in an especially good mood. Even in the morning, Baki's best friend, a herdsman named Senna, was already drunk and jolly, emerging from his ramshackle home to greet the farmer and his family. He knew that his festivities would be short-lived as there would be a herd that would need tending the very next day.

Down the road was a fisherman named Nefer, who was generously sharing pieces of smoked catfish. Next door to Nefer were two young widowed sisters, Tameret and Satmut, their husbands both killed on military adventures in Canaan. Both women were weavers, spinning flax, working the looms, and sewing at two cloth-producing facilities nearby. From Lower Egypt, they had met their spouses while the two soldiers from Thebes were on a prolonged stay up north. Now far from their own families, they seemed hopelessly sad. Despite their usually forlorn demeanours, the sisters responded this day with weak smiles to everyone who passed and acknowledged their existence. Mutui handed each a handful of dates from a little cloth bag she carried and their faces lit up with appreciation.

As they continued, Baki and his family passed by the homes of woodworkers, a jeweller, and makers and purveyors of all manner of crafts, and even some professional musicians and dancers. Being so close to Thebes, there were also numerous employees of the massive state bureaucracy that touched the lives of all, in one way or another. Several in the village worked in the households of the wealthy, many of whom were owners of extensive tracts of land or worked as high officials. Some of their exquisite villas lay directly behind the village, separated from those they considered lowly by their walls and gates.

Further along the way was the crude hut of Ahmosi, the amulet seller. No one knew her age but there were suggestions that she was as old as ninety, and had seen many generations precede her, and experienced the rule of several prominent pharaohs. With long, straight grey hair, bent over, and virtually no teeth, Ahmosi rarely wore clothes over her wrinkled body – perhaps she merely forgot to dress herself – but today she wore what appeared to be a dirty cloth sheet with a hole cut through its top. As usual, she sat in her doorway, a mat covered with her carefully arranged wares spread before her.

Seeing Baki, Ahmosi began to cackle and point at the array of amulets, many strung individually or in combinations to be worn around the neck; there was something to protect one from all manner of malevolent forces. Most were well-made of faience, a type of baked ceramic-like material with a lovely glassy green or blue glaze. At the edges of her mat stood some small statuettes designed for use in one's household. With his squat body, and ugly face with a long protruding tongue, the ever-popular Bes could be placed in a niche in one's house to ward off the undesirable. Baki's family already had three, and Mutui had a small figure of Taweret, a fierce pregnant hippo who was believed to provide protection during childbirth.

Although it was incredibly difficult to understand Ahmosi when she spoke, or gauge how much of her mind was intact, she knew how to sell her goods. As the children gawked at the delightful variety of colours, shapes and sizes representing one force or another, the old woman leaned over and put a loop of string over each of their necks from which dangled a small blue faience amulet. It was the *udjat*, the guarding eye of the god Horus. Not wishing to deny their children protection, Mutui reached into her bag of dates and removed a generous handful, Ahmosi moving her mouth in appreciation. 'No wonder she's survived this long,' muttered Baki as they walked away. 'She's surrounded by defensive beings!'

Nearing the end of the village road, a small plume of smoke could be seen in the near distance; obviously, someone was at work despite this day of celebration. The cloud was produced by a potter's workshop, which, thankfully, was situated far enough away to spare the local inhabitants from the acrid smell of the kilns.

Having traversed the village, it was now time for Baki's family to turn around to see how the festival was evolving. A few musicians were now playing flutes and a variety of small drums, while several members of the community engaged in a bit of impromptu dancing. A glance into a small gathering revealed a couple of men playing senet, a board game involving movable pieces. Nearby, several young men were wrestling, while others were competing in friendly matches of stick-fighting. A few little girls sat together, gleefully playing with dolls that more resembled small boat paddles with hair attached than real people, but the imagination of a child seemingly knows no bounds.

In mid-afternoon, a couple of donkey boys arrived with four huge jars that were carefully unloaded and set into a pile of supporting sand. It was the anticipated state-provided gift of strong beer that could be shared among the many. And later, an old cow, purchased communally, would be butchered and roasted on a spit for an infrequent and delicious treat for the village. Yes, it was the first day of the year, something to be celebrated, in terms of having survived the last, but also with hopes that the months ahead would be healthy, and at least somewhat happy.

# Second Month of the Season of the River's Flooding

## AMENHOTEP, THE RULER

Aakheperure Amenhotep stood naked and still as a servant poured a fixed number of jars of warm water over his body and then dried him off. Taking his place on a low chair, Egypt's king awaited the next to arrive, the royal manicurist and shaver. It was all too routine, the same process repeated identically day after day, year after year, whether in Memphis, Thebes or elsewhere. When the two men appeared, obsequious and fawning as usual, the ruler just wasn't in the mood to be examined carefully or scraped with razors, nor have his nails precisely maintained. 'Not today!' he ordered to their surprise and they backed away slowly. The perfume attendant came next to apply oil and sweet-smelling ointments, something Amenhotep barely tolerated.

In short order came the dresser, offering clothing suggestions appropriate for the day's schedule. 'How about a lovely tunic accompanied by a beautiful belt?' he asked, holding up a long, pleated white gown of the best linen, beautifully embroidered along the neck and down the front. The belt was red and embellished with gemstones.

'That will be appropriate,' responded the ruler with a degree of disinterest.

'And a sumptuous curly wig atop your royal head?'

'I have my own hair,' replied the annoyed pharaoh.

Indeed, Amenhotep didn't particularly like having his head shaved, and he found the wigs to be heavy and hot. 'I'll wear one of the diadems during the audience,' he ordered. The dresser offered no argument as he slipped the tunic over the king's arms and head, and tied the sash around his waist. Another attendant rushed in to apply a thick line of black make-up to accentuate the ruler's eyes, before standing back and smiling in admiration of his work. 'That's enough for now, you may leave,' Amenhotep concluded curtly, 'I'm going back to the bedroom for a bit more rest.'

Passing a guard, who pulled back the elaborate tapestry that served as a door, Amenhotep set himself on a fine and comfortable wooden chair with a footrest. Like most rooms in the palace, the royal bedroom was lit by horizontal slits high on the wall that let in sunlight during the day to be supplemented by oil lamps at night or when otherwise needed. And the walls were decorated with soothing geometric patterns and the ceiling painted to resemble a star-filled sky, an atmosphere with the possibility of providing calm and rest.

**AMENHOTEP II**

Amenhotep was tired. The cumulative effects of twenty-six years of the highest responsibilities along with the excesses of youth were taking their toll on his body, if not his mind. The well-being of Egypt depended upon his success in maintaining *maat*, that is, cosmic and civil order. As the ultimate high priest, the Egyptian ruler was charged with making sure that the gods were properly appeased, and that temples were built and maintained throughout the land, and that the proper rituals were performed. Obviously, he couldn't be present daily at all the temples, nor at the many festivals – there were extensive hierarchies of priests distributed throughout the land – but his presence was expected now and again including at the upcoming Opet Festival later in the month.

The ruler was also required to keep Egypt's enemies at bay. Once blessed with the security of natural boundaries that served to prevent incursions by invaders, there were now threats to the south and east to be deterred. In fact, just

## THE NAMES OF THE PHARAOH

The majority of the rulers of Egypt bore several names and titles. At birth, they were given a familiar name such as 'Amenhotep' and a throne name such as 'Aakheperure' was added upon becoming ruler. This throne name is quite important as it allows Egyptologists to distinguish between kings with the same birth names. There were, for example, multiple rulers with the birth names Amenhotep and Thutmose, and eleven with the name Rameses. These two names were written in hieroglyphs situated inside oval circles that scholars refer to as 'cartouches'. They are valuable in determining the date and ownership of many royal monuments and artefacts.

a few generations previously, Egypt had been taken over by eastern foreigners, the Hyksos, who had settled in the north, and then subdued the land, establishing themselves as the ruling power. Egyptian forces organized in Thebes were able to battle the outsiders and once again bring order and stability to Kemet. Although the Hyksos were vanquished, the Egyptians would not settle for merely ousting them. Instead, they would extend their authority to distant lands in the hope that they would never again fall under the dominance of a foreign power. The result was an impressive empire in which the fear of Egypt was spread, with tribute expected and booty demanded.

Amenhotep's father, the third ruler bearing the name Thutmose, pushed Egypt's dominance to its furthest extent thus far. With seventeen military campaigns conducted during his lengthy reign, the warrior pharaoh brought his might far into northern Syria and deep into Nubia, and the wealth extracted as a result was making Egypt ever more prosperous. With much of the foundation laid by his father, it was Amenhotep's responsibility as the supreme commander to make sure that the foreign lands behaved and provided what was demanded. Thus far, Amenhotep had needed to launch only three major campaigns during the course of his rule, although regular maintenance visits to the subdued regions were a necessity.

The first campaign took place when the people of Retenu refused to submit to Egyptian dominance and rebelled. With the terrifying Thutmose III dead, they greatly underestimated his successor and began to take advantage of the situation. Amenhotep demonstrated that he was very much a warrior as fierce as his father, and personally engaged in battle. In one of his legendary acts, he captured the seven chiefs of Takhsy in Syria and brought them back to Egypt. After hanging the chiefs upside down from the bow of his royal barque as it sailed triumphantly to Thebes, he personally killed them by bashing in their heads with a mace and then cutting off their hands. And for added humiliation, six of the corpses and their hands were displayed on the city's walls. The seventh putrefying corpse was then sent to Nubia as a warning.

**THE ROYAL NAME OF AAKHEPERURE AMENHOTEP WRITTEN IN HIEROGLYPHS ON A SCARAB AMULET (c. 1427–1401 BC) AND IN FULL**

A few years later, he led another campaign to Retenu in Syria, crossing the Orontes River, and punishing and plundering all who defied Egyptian dominance. He set off yet again two years later to pacify insurrections in Canaan during which he maintained his reputation for ruthlessness. In another act of profound cruelty, Amenhotep commanded that his prisoners dig a pair of trenches, fill them with flammable material, and stand within to await their fate. He then set them afire, and watched the horrendous spectacle, axe in hand in case any escaped the inferno. Knowledge of the ruler's propensity for extreme violence would spread, compelling those who might rebel to think twice. And Nubia and the Libyans were likewise dealt with as needed.

The door opened. It was Queen Tiaa who had gone about her own version of a daily bath and routine, her perfume almost more overwhelming than that of the pharaoh's himself.

Queen Tiaa was certainly beautiful and a fine mother, but Amenhotep noticed that she seemed to play favourites with their oldest surviving son, Prince Thutmose. Although the usual custom was that the oldest son would assume the throne of Egypt when his father died, Amenhotep had doubts about Thutmose. He seemed to be somewhat frail and effete, and while a couple of his brothers were training with the military, Thutmose was training horses, hunting and enjoying desert excursions

Quite the opposite, Amenhotep himself had a great reputation as an athlete, a fact that was known and promoted to everyone in Egypt. He was a great charioteer, an archer who could shoot arrows through thick ingots of bronze while on the move, and he could out-row, out-run and out-fight anyone, so it was said. The empire had to be maintained and there was little room for a weakling; it was something that had been weighing heavily on the king for some time.

Getting up from his chair, Amenhotep walked to his dining room where his breakfast awaited. As usual, the table was piled high with the best that Egypt had to offer. It was all too much, but fit for a god-king. It wouldn't go to waste; the numerous functionaries in the palace would make sure that it would be eaten elsewhere, and there would be even more with another elaborate banquet set for the evening. Tiaa and a couple of the princes had already eaten but they barely made a dent in the grandiose meal.

A GRANITE RELIEF FROM THE TEMPLE OF KARNAK DEPICTS
AMENHOTEP II AS A SUPER-ATHLETE, SHOOTING ARROWS THROUGH
THICK PLATES OF COPPER FROM A MOVING CHARIOT

The pharaoh had just finished a few grapes, some dates and some slices of roast duck – all slugged down with a large cup of beer – when an impeccably dressed portly gentleman entered the room.

Pairy was the nickname of Amenemopet who was not only Amenhotep's childhood friend, but served as the ruler's vizier, the right-hand man who could manage much of Egypt's daily affairs as a sort of overseer of the overseers. He met with the highest officials daily and afterwards provided a summary to the king.

## Visitors from the East

Amenhotep groaned as he arose. A palace functionary dashed out and gently placed a gleaming gold diadem in the form of a cobra atop the ruler's head, the snake's fanned hood appearing to almost leap out from the front of the crown, while its sleek body wrapped around the wearer's head. With Pairy in front, the two went into the audience hall where rows of seated scribes bowed in supplication as the pharaoh became visible. A couple of rows of daunting well-armed soldiers stood alert along the walls, their daggers and spears at the ready. With light streaming through the windows, oil lamps casting shadows, billowing clouds of incense, and a loud beating drum, the scene would assuredly intimidate anyone who might venture into the presence of the god-king.

The polished ruler took his seat on his stunning golden throne situated on a well-elevated dais, his sandals resting atop a low gilded platform embossed with the likenesses of Asiatics, Libyans and Nubians, symbolically vanquished under the ruler's feet. Two fan-bearers standing behind the throne – both trusted friends of Amenhotep – began to gently circulate the air, their devices bedecked with ostrich plumes. Tiaa's own throne was set back and off to the side, but her appearance was likewise stunningly regal. Pairy approached with a beautifully carved wooden box from which Amenhotep retrieved two gilded and bejewelled symbols of his power, a crook and a flail, letting all know his ability to be both a fatherly guide, and a ruthless punisher.

'Let them in,' ordered the ruler, and the two great wooden doors opened to admit several guests and petitioners. Accompanied on each side by armed guards and a translator if necessary, all would catch a brief look at the king before being ordered to kneel down on all fours and keep their noses to the floor until told to do otherwise. Amenhotep sat quietly staring through the haze of incense, the crook and flail crossed and motionless in his hands, his highlighted eyes glaring. The effect was intentional; all who had the rare privilege of being in the ruler's close presence would leave in astonishment, and would report their personal experience of awe to all who might listen.

Pairy stepped forth and began a loud introduction, which he knew from memory after hundreds of similar recitations. 'Behold! You are in the presence of the living Horus, the strong and mighty bull with sharp horns, one who is powerful in splendour when he appears in Thebes, one who uses his strength to seize all lands, the son of Re, AakheperureAmenhotep!'

The vizier announced the first petition. 'Iamunefer, High Priest of the Temple of Thoth in Khemenu of the Hare Nome, wishes to make a request.' The ruler nodded and the priest rose to his feet.

'Our temple needs repairs, our temple needs expansion. Thoth has been good to us and is deserving. May your divine majesty bless us with the resources for this project.' Amenhotep had already been advised of this request and the vizier had consulted with the Overseer of the Treasury. The decision had been made to approve. Without saying a word, Amenhotep gave a slow nod while glaring directly at the priest.

'Your request has been granted,' announced Pairy, and the priest was led backwards to the exit with his head bowed in gratitude.

Several other officials making similar requests came and went before Pairy ordered that the last visitors of the day be admitted. 'Next, a special gift from a distant land,' announced the vizier as a decrepit bearded man in a long striped robe entered with two young and modestly clad girls in ankle-length wool dresses. The three knelt down before being asked to rise. 'This man is named Yaacov and he is from a small town near Rekhesh. Arise all three of you, and your translator as well,' ordered Pairy. 'His majesty, the living Horus, the strong and mighty bull with sharp horns, one who is powerful in splendour when he appears in Thebes, one who uses his strength to seize all lands, the son of Re, Aakheperure Amenhotep, indeed well remembers the town and your people, which both he and his father punished, yet still refuses to submit.'

Yaacov began to speak as the translator repeated his words in Egyptian. 'I am the chief of a small town in Canaan. My people and I are greatly sorry for our unacceptable behaviour. You brought your mighty soldiers and we foolishly fought. We now will honour your greatness. Now we have very little but we will share with you what we have.' Amenhotep appeared bored with the apologies and accolades while the old man continued. 'I have brought you a very special gift: two of my daughters. They are both beautiful and a sign of peace between Egypt and my miserable town.'

Amenhotep was unimpressed. His father had been given several foreign wives from far more powerful families than that of a village chief, but nonetheless, it was a sincere gesture. Pairy knew exactly what to say in such a situation: 'His divine majesty, the living Horus, the strong and mighty bull with sharp horns, one who is powerful in splendour when he appears in Thebes, one who uses his strength to seize all lands, the son of Re, Aakheperure Amenhotep, accepts your gift. They will be bathed, perfumed, well fed, well clothed, and housed in the harem where they will be taught to sing, dance and be pleasing.' The two demure girls and their father began to shake upon hearing the translation. Several soldiers stepped forward to escort the three out of the hall and all were led off quietly weeping

'That is enough,' whispered the pharaoh to Pairy, who announced to all that the audience was over. With the diadem removed from his head, and his stately props replaced in their cases, the ruler of Upper and Lower Egypt returned to his bedroom to anticipate his many obligations to come in the following weeks.

## OFFICIALS OF THE REALM

Ancient Egypt's sophisticated society was managed by a vast bureaucracy composed of an enormous number of state officials, including specialized overseers and directors, inspectors, scribes and accountants who supervised or were otherwise involved in nearly everything, from granaries to ladies of the harem. In the royal household there were numerous attendants to address the ruler's every need, including physicians, stewards, fan-bearers, sandal-bearers and overseers of the wardrobe. All of these government employees and their activities had to be subsidized, and taxation of the general population and the wealth brought in from subdued foreign lands helped to pay the expenses.

## The Opet Festival

It was the fifteenth day of the month and everyone in Thebes, at least, was anticipating the grand pageant that was about to begin. The city's population had greatly expanded with outside visitors, excited and anxious to experience something truly spectacular and awe-inspiring: the annual Opet Festival honouring the great god Amun, the god so dominant in the current successful affairs of

Egypt. For most of the non-priests in attendance, it would be the closest they'd ever be to the actual gods themselves, as the images of Amun, and his wife and son, Mut and Khonsu, made an annual journey from the magnificent temple to Amun, 'The Most Select of Places' (Karnak) to 'The Southern Sanctuary', another temple glorifying the god just to the south (Luxor Temple).

Intef woke up early that morning to join his fellow priests of Amun for their daily purification routines, shaving their bodies and thoroughly washing themselves before dressing in gleaming white linen kilts. Although it was a regular ritual, their sense of piety was especially enhanced with the knowledge of the importance of this day. Everything and everyone must be perfect. Intef normally served as a bureaucrat in Memphis for all but a month of the year, at which time he had the honour of serving as one of numerous similarly rotating priests. This was his first turn in Thebes, and his first Opet Festival.

The sun had barely risen and it was time for the High Priest of Amun, Amenemhat, and his most senior of assistants to service the god, making their way through courtyards and a set of increasingly small chambers in Amun's temple, where the god awaited to be honoured, fed and clothed. Piles of food were laid out on tables in front of the last room and the aroma of expensive incense wafted throughout. Approaching a tall shrine, Amenemhat unsealed and opened its doors to reveal the statue that Amun himself inhabited. Still wearing the unguent-soaked linen from the previous night's ritual, Amun was carefully undressed and washed, reclothed and readorned, while the assisting priests chanted their praises outside. It was a ritual that took place twice daily, but today, Amun would be having his supper elsewhere.

Amenemhat closed and sealed the wooden shrine and called for half a dozen priests to step forward to aid in picking up the heavy box and very gently transferring it to a sturdy wooden litter. Thus accomplished, the shrine was carried out to a courtyard to be installed on its manner of conveyance for its journey: a large and ornate wooden barque on whose deck the god's shrine would sit. Long wooden poles ran along the base of the boat, a ship that would be making its initial journey on land.

With all secured, Amenemhat proceeded to an even larger courtyard of the temple where hundreds of sparkling clean priests awaited. 'This is the festival of Opet!' he loudly announced. 'And our great god, Amun, will be honoured and celebrated in the most grand and sacred manner.' Intef was awe-struck even before the grand moments were to begin. 'Today,' continued the high priest, 'a dozen strong men will carry Amun in his barque for a couple of hours on a journey south. The barque is heavy and cannot be dropped. You will not drop the barque of Amun!'

Immediately, one of the senior priests ordered that all line up by size. A dozen tough men of similar physical stature would be needed to carry the barque on its terrestrial voyage. Intef had mixed feelings. Although it was an incredible honour to transport the god, it was likewise an intimidating prospect. Apart from the physical labour, it would be crowded and noisy, if not a bit chaotic.

Amenemhat strolled along the ranks until he found a row of priests of identical height, some smiling while others looked quite stoic. Amenemhat pointed out Intef and all but the selected dozen were dismissed to take their places in the outermost courtyard where everyone was assembling in preparation for Amun's dramatic departure from his home.

Intef and his team of barque-bearers were led back to the boat to be given their instructions by one of the senior priests. 'The barque will be lifted and carried steadily and gently. Never forget, Amun is on board! Amenemhat will walk slowly in front of you and you will walk at the same pace. There will be much going on but you must concentrate on your task. There will be some in the crowd that will seek wisdom from Amun by hoping to detect any indication of an answer from a stray movement of the barque. Do not be distracted by their shouts. The barque is very heavy but there will be several places to rest along the way. And do not forget: the Lord of Upper and Lower Egypt, the living god, Aakheperure Amenhotep himself, will be in attendance. Do not disappoint the ruler and do not disappoint Amun! Do not drop the barque!'

With the firm orders given, the priests approached the barque, Intef struggling to contain his fear. Six sturdy priests lined up on each side and, on command, lifted the shrine-bearing boat in unison, placing its carrying poles solidly on their shoulders. Amenemhat appeared, taking his place in front, leading into the outermost courtyard where a huge crowd of parade participants were organized and ready. With the appearance of the barque, the grand

**Priests carry the barque of Amun during the Opet Festival**

procession was about to begin, with the sounds of drums and music, as all exited the temple.

Up front was a group of well-armed soldiers surrounding the horse-drawn chariot of the pharaoh, protecting him from the mob lining the processional path. Then came a contingent of chanting and singing bald-headed priests, some bearing incense to please their god. Next came the barque and its bearers, accompanied by more soldiers and dozens of musicians and dancers. Given the slow pace, several of the dancers were able to perform flips and other difficult gymnastic moves, which added a special joyful element to the proceedings.

Thousands of Egyptians from every walk of life lined the procession, excited to see Amun, or at least his shrine, and perhaps even catch a glimpse of the ruler. There were groups of bureaucrats dressed in their finest, and common workers in clothing still smudged from their morning's labour. Baki the farmer was there with his family, lifting high his young son to gain a view of the spectacle. As warned, there were a lot of shouts from the watching crowd. 'O great god, Amun! Is my wife pregnant? Show me a sign!' Someone else yelled out, 'Will my son be married this year?' A fly flew into Intef's face, producing a flinch that caused a minute lurch in the barque while he squinted in helpless annoyance.

## KARNAK

The building of the Karnak temple complex began during the reign of the Middle Kingdom pharaoh Senusret I (c. 1950 BC). Subsequent rulers added to it for almost two millennia and today it covers an area of over 247 acres (100 hectares) with an abundance of columns, pylons, statuary, a sacred lake, and obelisks. Karnak is considered the largest religious complex in the world and includes temples dedicated to the god Amun and his wife, Mut, and his son, Khonsu, along with structures dedicated to various rulers. A ceremonial causeway lined with ram-headed sphinxes connects it to the massive Luxor Temple about two miles to the south.

As the procession moved on, those seeking divine advice reached their own conclusions with every perceived deviation of the barque.

Not too far away was a small temple for Amun's wife, Mut, where priests bearing a smaller barque with its own shrine joined in behind Amun, and the same followed with a visit to the temple of Khonsu, their son. With all of the sensory overload and the weight of the boat, Intef was already becoming weary. Fortunately, a platform of perfect height for setting the poles down was soon met, and after a short rest, the procession would continue to its destination. Soon enough, the sight of the columns of the southern temple loomed near, and with great jubilation in its courtyard, the barque of Amun was brought within its walls finally to be set down in its well-prepared setting. It was soon joined by Mut and Khonsu as the divine visit south ensued.

Intef was incredibly relieved with a feeling of success and honour, and the group of twelve rested and congratulated each other. Although the journey had taken only a couple of hours, there were plenty of anecdotes to share. One priest had been hit in the face by a large, ripe fig thrown from the crowd, while another had nearly tripped when one of the tumbling dancers crashed against his leg, and all had heard the various requests for answers from Amun. 'Amun, will my hair grow back?' was a favourite, and one of the priests admitted that he faced some of the truth-seekers and intentionally rolled both his head and his eyes, providing an ambiguous answer from the god.

Amun, Mut and Khonsu would remain in the southern temple for eleven days, being feted and celebrated daily. As the ultimate High Priest of Egypt, the ruler Amenhotep himself would actively participate, thus reinforcing his association with Amun, and rejuvenating his own divinity. Dressed, fed and anointed multiple times daily, the visiting gods presided over all, even if their images were still physically invisible to the majority of the participants.

## THE GENTLE SIDE OF A WARRIOR PHARAOH?

Ironically, despite Amenhotep II's reputation for viciousness when dealing with foreign adversaries, he was fond of some animals – especially horses – and appreciated flowers. His own father, Thutmose III, maintained a botanical garden and a private zoo. In 1906, three small undecorated tombs were discovered in the Valley of the Kings and found to contain the mummies of baboons, a dog and a few birds. The tombs were robbed in ancient times and the animals' mummies found inside were stripped of their wrappings by thieves in search of valuables. Although these burials are still a mystery, a popular idea is that they were the favourite pets of Amenhotep himself, interred in close proximity to the king's own royal tomb.

For the majority of the festival, Intef merely assisted as needed, as was his usual duty at Karnak, but the eleventh day did come and it was time once again for the appointed teams to convey the barques. The return trip, however, would be much different. As he lifted the carrying pole on to his still-bruised shoulder, Intef was relieved in the knowledge that their journey was only a short and careful portage to the banks of the river, where all three barques would be placed on a barge for an easy downstream journey back to their home temples. The barge would be accompanied by Amenhotep's own spectacular royal boat named *Aakheperure Is the Establisher of the Two Lands*, and cheering crowds would line the banks of the Nile. At Karnak, other barque-bearers would be anxious and nervously waiting. Opet was over, and Intef's annual duties at the temple were coming to an end. It had been an intense and successful festival, and most importantly, they didn't drop the barque of Amun!

# Third Month of the Season of the River's Flooding

## THE FISHERMEN

Nefer ambled his way down to the riverbank, a short distance from the simple shack he lived in on the high ground at the edge of Baki's wheat field. He didn't mind the humble accommodation: three ageing mud-brick walls with a roof of palm branches, a mat and blanket for sleeping and sitting, and a few folded clean skirts that served as a pillow. There was no need to wear clothes most of the time in his profession; life as a fisherman in the Nile was consistently wet, often muddy, and the stench of fish was persistent. Unmarried as yet, his life was thus far mostly uncomplicated, and his work reliable and mostly enjoyable, though occasionally dangerous. Drowning was always a possibility with the river's variable currents capable of exhausting even the strongest swimmer, and two of Egypt's most feared creatures – crocodiles and hippos – killed many a fisherman, and others, each year.

Nefer's own father and two of his brothers had met such a fate just a few years previously when the enormous head of an angry hippo emerged from the depths, mouth agape, and bit their flimsy fishing skiff through its middle. The beast's powerful jaws and sharp tusks delivered mortal injuries to all three on board. Nefer watched helplessly from the shore and there was little that could be done other than to scream and later retrieve the bodies downstream. Unlike the crocodile in its vicious and indiscriminate search for any fresh meat, the hippos ate vegetation, but their angry behaviour was considered sheer evil. Still, Nefer mostly enjoyed his occupation, and preferred it to what he perceived as the obnoxious aspects of almost every other profession. And there was always the possibility of a surprise, good or bad, each time he entered the water, thus adding a sense of adventure.

Reaching the Nile, Nefer was greeted by several of his friends sitting in the sand, repairing nets for the day ahead. Nefer loved working with this group, some of whom were his own cousins. They were all about the same age and employed by his uncle who made sure that the young men were well supplied with the necessities of life: bread and beer, and fish, of course, with most of the daily catch sold fresh in the market. 'We're going to have a good day and a big catch, if Hapi should be so generous!' proclaimed Nefer, and all agreed. The day's agenda was relatively easy: two teams of two would work together with nets from a pair of skiffs while the others would fish from the shore.

It was a rare day when nothing was caught. As their little boats lay at the edge of the water, the fishermen examined them carefully to make sure that all were in good order. Made from tightly bound bundles of buoyant papyrus stalks retrieved from the river's edge, a few knots were in need of tightening, including the pointed ends on each vessel, which were pulled up and down and tied to the floor of the skiff. The normal equipment aboard included a harpoon, a punting pole, a basket holding nets, and a wooden club. With all in order, a couple of loops of dried tied papyrus stalks were thrown aboard; they could be thrown over one's shoulder for flotation in the event of an emergency.

Once a few baskets had been loaded the two skiffs set out for the edge of the marsh, pushing off with their poles. Nefer would direct the nets today, supervising the positioning of the boats close to each other, and then tossing the nets between the two. The idea, of course, was to collect any fish that might wander by, but in reality, it wasn't always that easy. There was a lot of debris and floating vegetation in the river that could be captured, or could tear a net. And there were plenty of stories of odd things that had been caught: a palm tree, a bloated dead baboon, another fisherman's tangled net, and even a deceased villager.

Standing, balanced in the centre of the skiff, Nefer grabbed one edge of the net while his partner prepared the other. In well-rehearsed coordination, they tossed the net across to the other vessel where it was caught and held, the bottom edge sinking below the water. After patiently waiting for several minutes, the two little boats were punted to shore, and with the help of others, the net was pulled in and its catch examined. Among a tangle of sodden plants and a deceased ibis, a few small fish were flopping about. One of the men dispatched them with a wooden club before tossing them into a basket. Carefully, the net-throwers removed the debris before setting out once again.

Those fishing on shore with lines, too, were having moderate success, but further down was an old man who seemed to be a master of his craft. Nearly blind and working alone, Thanuny wandered the river's edge with a harpoon, and stared into the water with whatever eyesight remained. Exercising profound patience sometimes lasting dozens of minutes, he would eventually thrust his weapon into the water and, more often than not, pull in an exceptionally large fish. On some days, Thanuny would bring in a bigger catch than Nefer and his friends combined. They would watch in amazement and once asked the old man, his eyes white and glazed, if he might share any secrets. His answer seemed intentionally ambiguous: 'What I cannot see, I can hear, smell and sometimes feel. And I have patience.' Thanuny could expertly clean the fish with seemingly little effort before carrying a full basket away after a relatively short day.

With full baskets on their shoulders, the two fishermen headed across the dry elevated road to the village where the market was in full operation. Nefer's uncle had been waiting impatiently and made his usual expressions of disappointment as he examined the catch. Pulling out

**FISHERMEN AT WORK ON THE BANKS OF THE NILE**

the smallest fish from the baskets, he handed one to each of his employees and pointed to their consumable day's wage: some bread loaves and a couple of jars of beer on a nearby mat. 'I expect more tomorrow,' was his usual dismissive response.

## THE FARMER IS DRAFTED

With his chores relatively light while the Nile still flooded the fields, and the temperature pleasantly warm with a friendly breeze, Baki strolled down the village street feeling content and looking forward to a noontime meal and a nice nap. Just a short distance from his own house, the farmer stopped in his tracks, looking for another option to reach his home. Two men were standing at a neighbour's door having an angry conversation with the occupant. One was dressed in the immaculate clothes of a palace or government official, while the other wore a short skirt and carried an intimidating spear in his hand, and a short dagger at his side.

Taking a route across the edge of a couple of soggy fields, Baki kept low as he reached the edge of his house and rushed inside. Pulling back slightly the sheet that served as his doorway, he caught a glimpse of the two outsiders making their way in his direction. 'If the men come here, tell them I'm away,' he ordered his wife. 'Tell them that I broke my leg and I'm recovering at the home of a relative in a distant village!'

'I'll do no such thing,' responded Mutui. She was well aware of the situation that was occurring nearly every year. The two men were government officials announcing the conscription of farmers and others who might be seasonally lightly employed. Two men would appear, one a scribe bearing the official news, and the other a soldier whose very appearance was intimidatingly persuasive. The previous year, Baki had been sent away for several weeks to help build an enormous granary a day's sail away to the north. The work wasn't that hard, mostly passing sun-baked bricks from one man to another, to be ultimately set in place by masons, but it was tedious and boring.

All of the conscripts slept in the most basic of barracks with each night accompanied by the snoring and other obnoxious sounds emanating from their fellow workmen. The food was plentiful but bland, as was the beer, and with all of the mud and mortar involved, it was hard to stay clean. Baki acknowledged, though, that no one was particularly mistreated unless they were uncooperative or tried to leave their job; all of the permanent project supervisors were well aware that most of their additional help were recruited farmers taking time away from their families. If there was anything truly dangerous or severely arduous, there were always prisoners or foreign captives to deal with such tasks.

Baki could see the two emissaries coming close to his door and ran to his sleeping mat before pulling a blanket over his head. Only moments later, the expected voice was heard. 'Greetings, friends. We are here to speak with Baki the Farmer. Is this the home of Baki the Farmer? Is Baki here?' Mutui pulled back the door to greet the visitors. The one speaking was clearly a scribe and was holding a sheet of papyrus with a long list of names, while the armed man stood silently to the side.

'This is the house of Baki,' she replied while her husband remained quiet and hiding with hopes of not being detected nor engaging in conversation. '. . .and Baki is right here, taking a nap!'

The farmer gave his wife a sneer as he arose to respond to the two men standing in his doorway, unconvincingly blinking his eyes as if he had actually been sleeping. The fact was that, although she appreciated her husband most of the time, Mutui did enjoy a bit of time without him, especially when he spent too much time around the house during the season of flooding. 'Greetings, O Baki!' effused the scribe. 'You probably know why we are here. On behalf of our majestic ruler, Aakheperure Amenhotep, his esteemed vizier, Amenemopet, and the Overseer of Royal Works, Benia, your abilities will be needed for the supreme honour of assisting with the construction of his majesty's House of a Million Years.'

Baki stifled a groan. He knew that it was an elaborate memorial temple that had been under construction for some time and would serve as the eternal venue for the memory and adoration of the current pharaoh after his death. It sounded like another project passing bricks back and forth. On the other hand, it was nearby, just on the other side of the river in the area of several other such temples, and he could almost see the site from his home. Baki knew better than to refuse but asked a few questions:

'When do we begin? How long do you need my help? May I come home each night?'

'We will need you for four weeks, and as our work fills the day, we will have comfortable accommodation and good food for you and your fellow men, and your family will be provided with ample grain and beer in your absence. Please meet us tomorrow at dawn at the pier in front of the palace for the trip across the river. Rest assured that your work will honour the gods.'

## THE POTTER

Roy loved to make pots. Even as a small child he would play in the mud, forming increasingly more sophisticated miniature vessels that even impressed his father, who like his own father, and previous generations, was a potter by profession. Whereas Roy's father grumbled constantly about his repetitive, monotonous work, his son seemed to enjoy it with a kind of enthusiasm that appeared odd to most. Arriving at the pottery workshop early each and every day, he worked with few breaks – only taking time to chomp on some bread and swig down some beer.

Roy worked for the wealthy owner of the workshop, which produced jars and vessels of all sizes and varieties to hold beer, wine, oil, grain or anything else requiring transport or storage. They would always have work; even the best-made pots would likely break at some point as the piles of sherds outside any village could attest. And there were ample supplies of raw materials nearby to keep the operation going indefinitely.

Roy rarely spoke, and his supervisor knew better than to interrupt the ceramic prodigy whose work was unsurpassed. Twenty-five years old and still living at home with his parents, Roy remained unmarried, and there were those who joked that if he ever found a wife, she would be a clay pot. Most of the past week had involved producing several hundred globular pots with handles, something not particularly difficult but still requiring skill and a bit of concentration.

The process began with acquiring clay, which was readily available from deposits near the banks of the Nile, or from sources near the edge of the desert. The facility where Roy worked collected from both, and an especially good supply could be found in a corner of Baki's field. In return for its use, the farmer received a steady supply of surplus pots with which he could barter for other things. Several young boys were charged with collecting the clay, and then letting it soak before adding sand or other temper and mixing it well. When the material reached the correct consistency, it was formed roughly into balls and delivered in baskets to the potters.

The boys seemed always covered from head to toe in mud from their efforts, but Roy barely noticed as he suffered a similar fate. Sitting before a horizontal stone wheel set into a small pillar with a socket, he grabbed a glob of clay and expertly began the process. Wetting his hands in a jar of water from time to time, he spun the wheel with his left hand while forming the pot with his right. In just minutes, a well-formed body of uniform thickness was created, and the vessel was left to dry a bit as handles were attached to the outside. While pliable and still intact, decoration could be added or a wash of colour applied, but in the mass production of utilitarian wares such as this, it was deemed unnecessary.

Nearby, a large kiln made of mud brick was being prepared and the unfired pots were carefully positioned inside from a hole in the top. With a fire started beneath, the hole in the roof was closed up, and after a specific time, the finished solid jars were allowed to cool before being lifted by their now-solid handles and stacked nearby. Although he had produced untold thousands of pots, Roy always stood back in admiration at his products when they emerged from the kiln. The pots made from the Nile's sediment nearly always came out brownish or even red, while other clays might produce light hues.

## POTTERY AND ARCHAEOLOGY

The remains of complete and broken pottery items provide invaluable information to archaeologists investigating ancient Egypt and elsewhere. Pottery was a common and essential product in most ancient civilizations. Ceramic pots and jugs, bowls, plates and cups, had a myriad of uses as they do today, and they were regularly broken and replaced. Just as styles of clothing and furniture have regularly changed in modern days, so did pottery through the ages. A knowledge of pottery styles through time can help experts determine the general or specific dates for sites or parts of sites, even when little else remains.

With his insatiable desire to produce more pots than his associates, and of consistently higher quality, Roy would regularly continue working late after everyone had gone home. Occasionally, he would tackle some special projects, the latest being a jug with a spout in the form of the god Bes, ugly face and all. It was to be a gift for his mother, who unlike his pot-detesting father, would be surprised and delighted. The process required much more skill than spinning on a wheel, and most of the piece was formed from the inside out. Reaching through the top, Roy carefully formed Bes's grotesque features by pressing outward and adding a few more dramatic details with bits and pieces of clay applied to the outside. Bulging eyes, a dangling tongue and a scraggly beard were required along with some careful painting before its trip to the kiln. Functional and artistic, it would no doubt be a prized possession to his mother.

One night while working late a couple of years previously, Roy's work was interrupted by a man who introduced himself as 'Wah', who asked the potter if he could produce a few special jars for him once in a while. Wah removed a large pot hanging in a net from the side of his accompanying donkey and set it on the ground. 'Not Egyptian!' exclaimed Roy.

'You are correct,' replied Wah. 'It is from elsewhere,' he continued, 'but I find this style very attractive. Create some pots like this for me, and in return, I'll bring you some nice wine that you can share, or not share, with your friends and family.' Roy examined the curious light-coloured vessel with handles. Indeed, it was different, but by no means beyond his abilities. 'Can you make ten of these for me?' asked Wah as he passed the potter some wine in a nice cup. Roy swallowed it back and returned the cup for more. After a few refills, Roy agreed, and Wah would become a regular after-hours customer.

## THE PRINCE

The cool desert air moderated the heat of the sun as the two horsemen approached the dazzling, stupendous monuments. Thutmose climbed down from his steed and handed the reins to his guard. Holding his hand up to his eyes while squinting from the reflective glare, the young prince stared raptly at the three massive stone pyramids constructed by his distant royal ancestors. Visible off in the distance north from Memphis, these pyramids were not like the others found in Egypt. Although there were a good number to be found in the region, nothing compared in size and impressiveness, and some of the more recent ones further to the south of the capital had been cheaply made with cores of mud bricks, which already showed signs of physical deterioration.

To the dismay of his father, who felt the prince had more important things to do, Thutmose visited the area frequently. The largest pyramid, that of Khufu who had ruled Egypt over a thousand years previously, was towering, and like its neighbours, surfaced with gleaming polished limestone. The body of the god-king Khufu was interred inside, protected from human predation by the pyramid's sheer mass. The monument's shape seemed to focus the rays of the sun like a stairway to heaven, and resembled the primeval mound from which the god Atum arose to create the lives of gods.

Khufu's monument was closely matched in size by that of his son Khafre, who built his pyramid on slightly higher ground to appear taller than that of his father, although Khafre's is marginally of lesser dimensions. The third pyramid belonged to the ruler Menkaure. Although much smaller compared to its two neighbouring predecessors, it is still incredibly impressive with its base utilizing red granite from the far south of Egypt as casing blocks. Six diminutive pyramids in the vicinity are said to contain the burials of queens or princesses, and all around were hundreds of squat rectangular structures, arranged in rows, which served as the private tombs of numerous royal officials and friends from distant times.

Situated at the base of each of the three large pyramids were temples where offerings were once presented in days long past, and stone-paved causeways led to other temples, which were likely used during the funerals of these particular rulers. Thutmose struggled to calculate how many people and how much time must have been involved.

## THE GREAT PYRAMID

The Great Pyramid of Khufu at Giza, outside modern-day Cairo, covers an area of about 4.86 hectares (13 acres) and once stood 146.5 metres (481 feet) tall, with each side of the base being 230.6 metres (756 feet) long. Built around 2550 BC, it has been estimated that over 2 million cut stones were used in its construction and the project might have involved many thousands of workmen over a period of twenty to twenty-five years. Many of the workmen may have been farmers conscripted during the Nile's annual flood stage. It was the tallest man-made object on earth until its height was surpassed by the 160-metre (520 feet) spire of Lincoln Cathedral in England, completed in 1311.

It must have been a spectacular sight, with thousands of people pulling and placing heavy stone blocks to a precise plan. The young prince had gained an impression of the size of the operation when the wind would occasionally reveal the remains of mud-brick walls of a huge village of pyramid workmen, which like nearly everything else in the vicinity was unmaintained and sand-encumbered.

At the least, there had been a need for food and accommodation for a huge number of men, necessitating bakers and bakeries and other food providers, and dormitories for the workers, and physicians to treat the numerous injuries that must have been incurred. Just as now, with the large number of farmers idle during the annual flooding of the river, a workforce could readily be gathered to assist the full-time professionals. The inundation would also provide the bonus of bringing barges closer to the work-site, especially when quarries on the opposite side of the river were used.

With his endless fascination with the site, Thutmose loved to perambulate the great monuments, circling each pyramid, his guard and the horses following. The young prince saved his favourite monument for last, a giant Sphinx carved into the bedrock representing the ancient ruler Khafre as a manifestation of the sun god, Horemakhet, with the body of a recumbent lion, and the head of that king. Alas, only the Sphinx's gigantic head remained above the sand, its royal headdress and beard augmenting an impenetrable stare to the east. Built into a channel excavated into the rock, nature had buried its body.

**The Great Pyramid and the Great Sphinx partially buried in the sand on the Giza plateau. The Sphinx was not fully uncovered until the 1920s**

Though ancient, the Sphinx was still considered relevant, and Aakheperure Amenhotep himself had built a small temple with a commemorative stele nearby several years previously. Built mostly of mud brick, enhanced with limestone blocks and lintels, the monument was situated on the flat limestone bedrock of the plateau with its doors dramatically framing the Sphinx's great head.

It was early afternoon, and the young prince laid out a mat next to Khafre's neck and enjoyed a lunch of choice vegetables, some duck meat and a small jar of wine. It wasn't long before he dozed off; his guard keeping a distance while remaining alert. The dream that occurred during the prince's nap was both profound and prophetic. The Sphinx as Horemakhet appeared and offered a promise. In return for removing the sand encumbering his body, the god would assure that Thutmose would rule. Awaking with a start, the prince mounted his horse and began the return journey to Memphis in the south, the dream dominating his every thought.

In the Memphis palace, Amenhotep was displeased that Thutmose was again off on his own frivolous agenda, wasting time while there was much to learn if one were to eventually rule. The king was on the verge of a profound decision: perhaps another one of his strong, competent and serious sons, though younger, should be his successor. He would make such known soon, and although there would be questions among the people, it was likely to be for the good of Egypt. The pharaoh had brought the idea to the attention of Queen Tiaa who strongly objected. It was clear that Thutmose was her favourite, especially after the death of his brother Webensenu, who was also cherished by Amenhotep. The ruler's grief had been such that he had the prince interred in a small chamber in the royal tomb still under construction near Thebes.

Thutmose handed over his horse after he and his guard passed through the palace gates. Walking briskly to his mother's bedroom, he enthusiastically broadcast the story of his dream, a tale that brought Tiaa a degree of reassurance, yet at the same time inspired a sense of doubt. It would take more than a young man's dream to convince his father that his instincts were to be dismissed. Tiaa shared the story with her husband and his reaction was as she suspected it would be. Despite his complicity with the gods of Egypt, Amenhotep would not be swayed by such a revelation.

# Fourth Month of the Season of the River's Flooding

## THE SCRIBES

Minnakht walked down the long dusty road heading towards the river, followed by a young man, the tracks of their leather sandals distinct in the dust among all the bare toes and heels. Following obediently behind was a donkey with a leashed monkey on its back and a tethered goat close behind. The accomplished scribe was on a mission that day to procure a supply of high-quality paper for his use in the palace. Ordinarily, he would send an envoy, but his young apprentice, Dagi, was new and needed to learn the process. The novice would enjoy seeing the process of paper-making, Minnakht hoped, but more importantly, he needed to learn to assess quality and understand pricing.

Dagi, the son of a royal official, had recently finished scribal school and was pleased that his superior was thus far good-natured, which was certainly not the case with some of his classmates. One friend was employed by a bureaucrat in charge of building supplies for the great Amun temple in Thebes and was regularly given a swift kick accompanied by a rude rebuke for any perceived error in writing. Arguing that all was indeed correct was fruitless, and the result was the same either way.

It took several years to be competent in the Egyptian scripts and the process of learning was rigorous. Only a tiny fraction of the population could read or write and having those powers was a great responsibility requiring both accuracy and integrity. And it was a profession

## HIEROGLYPHS

Egyptologists refer to the formal Egyptian script as 'hieroglyphs' not 'hieroglyphics', which although in common use is really an adjective describing a pictorial script. Although it was tempting for early scholars to try to read the hieroglyphs as a kind of story-telling, a major breakthrough in understanding came when it was realized that the complicated Egyptian script actually represented sounds and words in a language. Because this writing system didn't indicate many of the vowels, Egyptologists still aren't sure exactly how it was pronounced.

for the elite or the children of the elite; rare was the literate farmer, although their other abilities were not to be dismissed.

Scribal school could be brutal, depending on the teacher, with the possibility of a harsh whack of a stick administered to those making mistakes or perceived as distracted or otherwise inattentive. Seated on the floor with their legs crossed, their taut linen skirts serving as a desk, the students learned to write hundreds of signs and the words composed of them. Both the formal and cursive versions of the script were to be mastered, with the latter being the most useful for everyday purposes.

Dagi's instructor wouldn't allow the students anywhere near good paper until near the end of their instruction. Up to that point, writing practice was typically on the surface of ubiquitous pot sherds found strewn on the outskirts of any village. Alternatively, one might use thin slabs of limestone with their nice white surface, which might reveal any errors or sloppiness when black, and occasionally red, ink was applied with the point of a sharpened reed stick. Occasionally, some cheap, used, or damaged paper was brought in upon which students could write on whatever blank areas were present.

The two scribes continued down the road, Dagi's writing kit slapping lightly against his side. He considered it to be a real treasure, a gift from his parents at finishing his instruction. It consisted of a rectangular wooden box of polished wood with a compartment within to hold several reed pens. Its exterior bore two circular depressions, one for each colour of ink. Hung from a cord across his shoulder, it indicated to all that an educated man of distinction was in their midst.

'What was your favourite exercise, Dagi?' enquired Minnakht. Much of the learning process was not only the repetitive drawing of signs and words, but also the copying of tales that were often entertaining, if not overtly instructive.

'The Shipwrecked Sailor! Such a great story!' came the enthusiastic reply.

'Mine as well,' responded the senior scribe.

The story revolves around the sole survivor of a shipwreck who finds himself on a strange island dominated by a giant talking snake bedecked with jewels and precious metals. The snake consoles the castaway and shares his own story of catastrophe and personal loss. In the end, the survivor returns home as the mysterious island disappears.

'When I was younger, I actually believed it was true. I'm not so sure now,' admitted Dagi.

'Ever copy the adventures of Sinuhe?'

'Over and over!'

'Did you learn anything?' asked Minnakht who knew the story all too well. A palace official named Sinuhe panics and flees from Egypt after learning the ruler he served has died, and then spends many years living elsewhere and behaving heroically, while yearning to return to his beloved homeland. He eventually does and is given a joyous welcome.

'I would conclude that he should never have left Egypt, the only good place. I can't imagine living anywhere else. And you know what I also learned in school? It's good to be a scribe!'

Minnakht laughed and began a recitation of one of the writing exercises that had been drilled into both of them; some of them preaching morality while other lessons were designed to convince them that their study efforts were worthwhile in comparison to nearly every other occupation, most of which were portrayed as utterly miserable.

'O scribe! Don't be lazy! Don't be lazy or you will be soundly chastised! Do not set your heart on pleasures or it will ruin you! Write with your hand and read with your mouth. Ask advice from knowledgeable people. The ear of the boy is on his back, and he will listen when beaten.'

'And by the way,' continued Minnakht, 'everyone but us is weary or in pain or smells bad: carpenters, potters, farmers, weavers, fishermen, masons, barbers and all the rest! As we were taught, "you'll love the scribal arts more than your mother!"'

Dagi joined in the classic mantra, and after a few minutes of frivolity, the two reached a marsh thick with papyrus plants growing near the river's edge. The sprays from the tall slender plants rustled in the pleasant breeze as a few shore birds skittered at the edge of the water. It was a busy scene with several workshops taking advantage of the versatile sedges that could be transformed into many useful things, including, of course, paper.

'I'm looking for Tati,' Minnakht announced to one of the workmen who then quickly left to find his supervisor. Minnakht took advantage of the wait to explain things to his protégé. Walking to a flat open area, he pointed to several men busy with knives and others wielding wooden pounders. Moments later a couple of naked fat men emerged wet and muddy from the swamp with great bundles of cut papyrus stalks bound to their backs, which they quickly deposited on the ground nearby.

'This is how paper is made,' explained Minnakht. 'The men with the knives are going to remove the green outside skin of the stalk and then make thin strips out of the white material inside.' Dagi was impressed at how utterly uniform the slices were in their thickness and length. Moving over to an area covered with flat stones, the description continued:

'These men are laying out the strips one next to the other with their edges overlapping and then another layer will go at a right angle across the first, also with their edges overlapping. You can see that they are the size of our usual paper. Next, they will pound the strips and this

**MEN AT WORK IN A MARSH, HARVESTING AND PROCESSING PAPYRUS PLANTS**

will bind them together, and after drying, paper is made!' Several workers were actively striking the layers with wooden pounders, and off to the side were several finished examples drying in the sun. Single sheets were useful for numerous purposes, and they could be cut into even smaller sizes. Long accountings or even funerary texts could be accommodated by gluing the edges of several sheets together and then rolling them into a scroll.

'Minnakht!' exclaimed an approaching man wearing a dirty skirt. 'What can I provide for your important work?'

'I would like one hundred single sheets along with twelve scrolls of standard length.'

The paper purveyor led the scribes into a room with tall stacks of single sheets on the floor and baskets of scrolls of different lengths. Minnakht grabbed a random sheet and held it up to the sun. 'Look, Dagi. It's perfect. No gaps and the surface is beautifully smooth.'

'You know that I make only the best,' assured Tati. 'Only for you.'

'Good! How much do I owe you?'

'Twenty-six deben. What do you have of that value?'

'I brought what you suggested last time and did not forget.'

Tati spied the donkey with its baggage and gasped. 'You brought a goat and a monkey! Thank you!' The vendor had indirectly made it known to Minnakht during a previous visit that he'd like a tasty goat for a celebration a few months ahead. As for the monkey, it could be exchanged with a specific local craftsman for a sturdy well-made chair. 'His children will love it!' Tati explained.

## PAPYRUS

The papyrus plant (*Cyperus papyrus*) is strongly identified with Egypt, most notably as the material used for the production of paper. The plant, however, had many other uses. It could, for example, be used to manufacture such things as baskets, shoes and ropes, and its stalks could be used to build buoyant river skiffs. Egypt's paper was highly desired and widely distributed in the Mediterranean region, especially during the time of the ancient Greeks and Romans. With environmental changes over the centuries, the plant is nearly extinct in Egypt today, although it still thrives in parts of central Africa. Papyrus was reintroduced to Egypt in the 1960s for the purpose of producing tourist souvenirs in the form of sheets of paper decorated with Egyptian themes.

While the paper order was being filled, Minnakht took Dagi to observe some of the other industries in the vicinity. A couple of rope-makers were busy pounding whole papyrus stalks into long flat strands before twisting and combining them to produce single thick cables of varying diameters. Nearby was a seated man artfully using strips discarded by the paper-makers to create sandals – luxury items, if not a sign of wealth.

## A Visit to a Wine-Seller

With the paper loaded into baskets suspended across the donkey's back, one on each side, Minnakht and Dagi began the trek to their next destination: a wine-seller. Minnakht had been invited to a couple of celebrations that very evening and was typically well received, although he occasionally considered that maybe it was his dependable arrival with the fruit of the vine that made him so popular. The seller's establishment was soon reached, its doorway festooned with a bough of living grape leaves, its one-room interior packed with jars of various sizes and shapes. Behind the shop, two workmen were busy stomping their feet in a large vat full of bright red grapes to produce juice in preparation for the fermentation to follow. A small shrine to the appropriate god, Shezmu, stood against a short wall, its image observing, and hopefully bringing success to the project.

The proprietor, Wah, was well familiar with the customer. 'O scribe! What may I sell you today?'

**PICKING AND STOMPING GRAPES TO PRODUCE WINE**

'What do you have?'

'I have some delicious wine that just arrived from Canaan!' the vendor exclaimed, pointing to several large jars in the corner. 'As a refined man like you knows, it is very expensive, but worth it!'

'Anything cheaper?' asked Minnakht.

'Yes, if you'd like, I have as much local wine as you need. It is always good, but nothing special; however, it does improve after drinking several cups!'

The scribe leaned over and quietly asked, 'Do you have something similar to the cheap stuff that looks like it's from Canaan, but really isn't?' Wah understood perfectly and smiled as he led the scribe to a corner of the room with a couple of tall slender jars sealed with mud, each bearing

IDENTIFIABLE POTTERY FROM PLACES SUCH AS CANAAN
PROVIDE EVIDENCE OF FOREIGN TRADE WITH EGYPT AND THE
IMPORTS OF SUCH ITEMS AS WINE, OILS AND RESINS

an inked inscription in cursive hieroglyphs. 'Looks like Canaanite, tastes like Egyptian!'

'Good!' exclaimed Minnakht. 'I'll take them both and one of the expensive imports. Scratch a mark on the side of the local jars so I can tell them apart from the genuine Canaanite wine.'

'Mark the two jars,' ordered the vintner to a young boy who was obviously familiar with the procedure. 'And I'll take two of those scrolls and twenty sheets for all three jars of the best Canaan has to offer!' Dagi looked on with a sense of confusion and delight, but there was much more to come.

Turning on to the main road with their paper and wine, the two scribes headed towards their respective homes – Minnakht resided in a small villa, while Dagi lived quite well at the home of his wealthy parents. 'Go home and put on some nice, clean clothes. We're going to a couple of weddings this evening. Meet me at the house of Benia the Overseer of Works tonight as Re descends in the west.'

## A Party at a Nobleman's Villa

At the appointed time, Dagi appeared at the gate of Benia's villa. Beautifully attired guests were arriving, with many of the men wearing brilliantly white, pleated linen skirts and expensive shawls, and the women bedecked in jewellery and lovely dresses, with some sporting elaborate braided wigs. Music could be heard coming from inside and it was clear that the wedding feast was well underway. Minnakht soon arrived, his donkey in tow with three familiar wine jars suspended in nets from its sides. Benia ran forward to greet him.

'Benia, I bring to you a gift for the festivities. Dagi! Will you fetch the two special jars of Canaanite wine for our friend?' Dagi knew exactly what to do, and carefully removed the two marked vessels from the donkey.

'Canaanite wine!' exclaimed Benia. 'So delicious and so very expensive! You are a great and true friend, Minnakht.'

Two boys rushed out of the gate and grabbed the wine while the overseer escorted the scribes into a lovely walled courtyard with a small pool surrounded by several fruit-bearing trees. From there, a wide door led to a crowded room, with dozens of guests obviously having a merry time. A group of musicians were situated in one corner, with singing led by a blind harpist accompanied by others playing lute

## BUYING AND SELLING IN ANCIENT EGYPT

The ancient Egyptians did not make use of coins or other currency until around 500 BC. Instead, they engaged in barter or utilized a kind of exchange based on a unit of copper or silver known as a *deben*. Various products had a known value compared to the *deben* and the populace could trade goods accordingly. Many state 'salaries' were paid with the staples of bread and beer, which if not personally consumed, could also be exchanged for goods.

and flutes, and banging on drums. A trio of dancing girls gyrated in wild abandon, each clad in nothing more than a string of beads around their waists and decorative head bands; stopping now and then to flirt coyly with the guests.

Many in attendance were clapping and singing along to the music while the newly-weds sat side by side in ornate chairs on a small platform. Several tables along one wall were piled high with delicacies including choice cuts of sliced meats and an abundance of fruit.

It was clear that many of the guests were already drunk, and the dancing girls weren't particularly sober either. At one point, a young girl made the rounds, placing cones of scented perfume atop the heads of several guests, the waxy mixture melting into hair or wigs and producing a luxurious scent that improved the odour of the environment as the crowded room began to heat up.

After a couple of hours of enjoying the frivolity, Minnakht and Dagi thanked an inebriated Benia and gave their best wishes to the married couple, before making their way to the gate of the villa. The expected sound of retching by those who had overindulged could be heard in the courtyard as the two made their way through the gate and into the street. The scribe and his assistant were going to another wedding party in the village near the house of the herdsman, Senna.

Dagi gave a shudder. As a well-bred member of Egypt's elite society, the socially inexperienced young scribe viewed the villages as necessary for all the services their people provided, but no place to tarry, and their occupants not a source of friends.

**Musicians entertain at a party**

'How do you know this herdsman?' enquired the apprentice.

'A few years ago, my young daughter wandered away from our home and was lost for three days. Her mother and I were terrified. Senna found her lost at the edge of a wheat field, tired, dirty and hungry. He took her into his home and cared for her until he learned of her parents' home and returned her to us. He is a good man and we are forever grateful, and in return I have helped him with some problems involving taxes and land. His son is marrying a cousin from the same village. She's a basket-maker by profession and they just moved in together yesterday, and the celebration is tonight. I know that you might be a little nervous but I think you'll like it.'

## And a Party in the Village

It took half an hour to make the walk from Benia's villa to the village with a full moon illuminating the way. Not unlike the last venue, the noise of a boisterous party could be heard from a distance, with lots of laughing, shrieking and the loud beating of drums. Lacking sizeable homes, the festivities were taking place in the street and in a large vacant area between a couple of the mud-brick houses. Dagi felt very self-conscious as he approached the crowd, with all eyes seemingly focused on the two richly dressed individuals, and the music dying down at their appearance. What would a couple of scribes be doing in the village at this hour? Surely they weren't here to work!

Fortunately, Senna rushed out almost immediately and greeted Minnakht and Dagi with great enthusiasm. Minnakht introduced Dagi, and sensing the discomfort of the visitors, Senna turned to the crowd and loudly announced that the scribes were his special guests and within moments the party returned with fervour.

'And I have brought you some excellent libations from Canaan, for this celebration,' announced Minnakht. Senna was shocked with gratitude as Dagi fetched the genuine jar of imported wine from the donkey. 'This is so wonderful! Many, many thanks!' effused the herdsman, and with that, the two elite guests joined the joyous crowd.

Lit by the moon and a string of torches, the party was no less exuberant than that at Benia's villa, and was perhaps even more so. The music was no less pleasing with several flutes, a lute and some drums in the mix, and the expected naked dancing girls were no less entertaining as they shook sistra and clappers while spinning their way up and down the street. There was food, of course, including a large ox roasting on a spit from which choice chunks of beef were cut and distributed, and grilled fish, too, and plenty of fruit and cooked vegetables. Local beer was in abundance and the married couple were served the excellent Canaanite wine as they sat on a brick bench in front of their home, greeting and thanking well-wishers.

Baki the farmer, however, was fuming as he recognized Minnakht as the official scribe who had come to his home the previous month and announced his recruitment for national service. No wonder Senna's brother – also a farmer – was never asked to serve time during the period of flooding! 'I guess it pays well to find an official's lost daughter!' Baki concluded before forgetting his anger with another hearty slurp of wine.

It was getting late and both of the scribes were beginning to tire from their long and busy day. Although

Senna begged them to stay, it was time to go as the crowd divided to let the two depart from the village.

'So, Dagi. Which party did you enjoy most?' enquired Minnakht.

The young scribe thought for a moment before arriving at an answer. 'They were both crowded, noisy and the food was excellent. Benia's guests were obviously better dressed but the people in the village were clean, and enthusiastic in their own way. But I must say, the Canaanite wine at the village celebration was much better,' he concluded with a wink. At an intersection in the road, the two moderately inebriated bureaucrats went their separate ways to retire to their respective comfortable homes. It had been quite a learning experience, concluded Dagi: watching the production of paper and other papyrus products, bartering with a goat and a monkey, some 'interesting business' with a wine merchant, and two spirited parties. If only every day could be so amazing!

# First Month of the Season of Sowing and Growing

## THE SOLDIERS

The trek from Egypt had taken a few weeks, but it was relatively easy and uneventful. Hungry for adventure, the hundred or so soldiers under the command of Paser were ready and eager for whatever might present itself in the days ahead. They had already passed smouldering towns and caravans of captives and booty heading back west to the Nile. Paser seemed to know most of the commanders and greeted them as close friends. He had trod this path himself, every few years, as a necessary undertaking established over the last few decades by the likes of Thutmose III and the present ruler, Amenhotep himself. Even some of the princes would participate now and again to continue the family tradition.

Ahead lay the first town on the agenda, one of several on the list prescribed by his overseer, a general who had seen it all. Camping near a well, not far away from their first objective, the troops lit fires that served not only for light, warmth and cooking, but also to strike fear into the hearts of those they would meet in the morning. For many of the younger soldiers, this would be their first encounter with non-Egyptians, and sleep was elusive.

In the morning, after an Egyptian-style breakfast of bread and a few local vegetables, Paser called a gathering of his men to explain the day's activities. 'My soldiers,' he announced, 'our ruler's father, the third Thutmose, Menkheperre, subdued this land, and many others far beyond. He conquered them and took their wealth and made Egypt richer. They are vile Asiatics and they hate us. Do not feel compassion for them. They are not Egyptians. Their gods are weak and their morals are weak. Look at the way they live! They live in houses of piled rocks and they have no great mighty river to sustain themselves. They will give us what we want and we will return again and again to take from them.'

The commander knew the territory well. As a young man, he had accompanied Amenhotep on his triumphant sortie in Retinu during the seventh year of the ruler's reign. It was an incredible adventure with the conquest of numerous towns and a few major cities, many of which had rebelled after the death of Thutmose III, who had conquered them first. Amenhotep returned to remind them that Egypt's arm remained strong and those who were forced to submit would continue to submit.

Paser absolutely hated the Canaanites and virtually anyone non-Egyptian. His first experience in the region was both dramatic and traumatic. While patrolling through the very town they were about to address, which was seemingly pacified, he and a few fellow recruits were ambushed. Two of his companions had heavy stones dropped on them as they traversed an alley, and as Paser ran away, he was knocked down by a sturdy resident who vigorously tried to choke him to death. The fight ended quickly when Paser grabbed his sheathed dagger and stabbed his way out of the fight, only to find that the two others had perished. Upon regrouping with his platoon, he learned that his experience was not unusual, and his commander ordered that the town be razed, many of its inhabitants slaughtered, and whatever wealth it might possess collected.

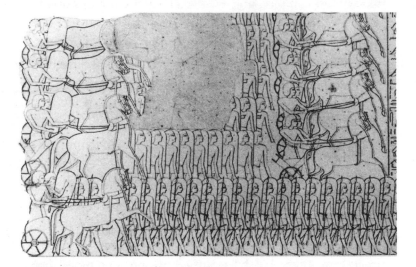

**Egyptian soldiers on the march!**

Paser continued his speech to the troops. 'The people you are about to meet are evil. We defeated them years ago but they quickly rebuilt. Do not trust them. We will ask them to give us whatever we like. I was here four years ago and they wanted to fight. We fought and they lost. Maybe it will be easy, but if they resist, they will lose once more. Our ruler, Aakheperure Amenhotep, was also here as a great warrior, and we will honour him with our strength and success.'

Despite the uplifting speech, many of the younger soldiers were now becoming nervous. While they awaited their orders, an Egyptian scribe fluent in the Canaanite language accompanied Paser and approached the town accompanied by a dozen experienced fighters bearing a variety of intimidating weapons. The town's chief, an elderly man named Shaul, emerged to face the Egyptians and actually recognized their leader. 'Paser,' he began. 'I know what you want and we are ready.' Shaul called forth a couple of young men who came out of a stone house struggling with two heavy baskets.

'What have we here?' enquired the commander as he inspected several layers of golden amulets and jewellery strung with beads made of polished gems. A more thorough examination, however, revealed that much of the weight of the basket was the result of the addition of ample sand and gravel in its bottom. Paser poured it on to the ground and immediately slapped Shaul harshly across the face. 'Bring me everything or you will have nothing!'

'But you were here only four years ago, and you took everything then. We have very little now,' pleaded the village chief.

Paser knew that Shaul's claim about the lack of goods was probably true, but the Egyptian empire required tribute and it wasn't always easy. Some of the conquered populations were complacent and met the approaching troops with an acceptance of reality. Everything attractive was pre-prepared and set out and the troops simply collected the tribute and moved on. In this town, though, the commander was nervous. Every one of his previous visits had ended with some sort of problem and, yet again, something seemed amiss. 'Search every home. Find anything of value.' The soldiers dispersed and most returned shortly with nothing in hand. One of the more thorough, however, emerged with a discovery.

'Look what I found hiding under a pile of wool!' With his finger thrust through her gold nose ring, a young teenage girl was pulled into the presence of his commander and thrown to the ground.

'So, there is some treasure! We'll have her, along with ten of your donkeys, thirty goats, and twenty baskets of grain along with your trivial jewellery.'

'Take me or kill me! Please don't take my daughter!' cried the girl's father.

'We will take her and we can kill you, but you are too old for us. Step aside,' replied Paser unemotionally, 'I'll take your son instead.' A young man stepped forward. He was immediately grabbed, his elbows bound painfully behind his back, and was then led off to be tied into what would be a growing line of captives. The platoon's accountant took note of all the new acquisitions as Paser gathered his troops to move on.

It was a disappointing haul, but understandable, concluded the commander. Even four years after the last visit by the Egyptians wasn't sufficient to recover and deliver the expected tribute. Still, the empire must be maintained, and the soldiers of pharaoh could only hope that the following towns would be similarly relatively docile, and hopefully more lucatrative.

With each 'visit' to a town on the agenda, the routine of intimidation continued. Donkeys, food, gold and other precious items of value were demanded and gathered, along with an attractive or strong inhabitant or two. The possibility of their complete annihilation was thus lessened, but not everyone was ready to submit. During the approach to the following village, one of the young Egyptian soldiers was violently struck on the side of the head by a rock launched from a sling. Although he lost consciousness, the accompanying military physician treated him effectively with experience based on many similar injuries.

As simple as it was, the sling could be a devastating weapon as wielded by many a Canaanite. Paser personally witnessed the event and on seeing the fleeing perpetrator, he called for his top archer who quickly and calmly pulled an arrow from his quiver. With calculations born of expert skill, he pulled his bow and let go. The projectile flew through the air in an arc, guided by proficiency and calculation, and the attacker was hit square between the shoulder blades.

The bowman turned to Paser. 'May I borrow your battle axe?' he requested. The commander handed him the weapon as the archer walked casually over to the twitching body. Placing one foot soundly on the man's back, he pulled hard on the arrow to retrieve it with its bloody, glistening bronze tip. Bronze was valuable, and arrow tips made from such materials were especially durable. Before leaving the body, the archer wiped off the blood on the victim's wool tunic, and then raised the axe, bringing it down on the dying rebel's right wrist.

## THE EGYPTIAN MILITARY

The ancient Egyptian army was formidable and its soldiers had an assortment of weapons at their disposal. Foot soldiers could be armed with bows and arrows, spears, daggers, hatchets, bone-crushing maces, and a devastating curved, sickle-like sword. Shields made from the tough hides of cattle stretched over a wooden frame provided some defensive protection. During the New Kingdom, the military adopted the use of the horse and chariot from some of their foes, and used them quite effectively. The ruler of Egypt was often shown drawing an arrow while leading his troops into battle in a chariot harnessed to galloping steeds. It's unknown to what extent pharaohs actually led the charge, but at least one mummy, that of the Theban ruler Seqenenre II, bears what appears to be a fatal axe wound to the head.

Picking up the severed hand by one finger, the archer slowly walked back to the assembled crowd of mostly subdued villagers and tossed the body part in front of all. Paser stepped forward. 'If anyone else wishes to defy the forces of the Strong Bull, Aakheperure Amenhotep, Lord of the Two Lands, Beloved of Amun, you will fail. This is the secret to your survival: you will continue forever to set aside anything of value for our taking when we return. And we will remember this village, and anyone who protests will be punished severely.'

## THE VIZIER

Amenemopet staggered up a rising trail along the Theban foothills, his feet slipping now and again on the loose limestone chippings produced from the construction of several tombs above, including one being built for himself. He had had a very busy day, and his lack of energy didn't surprise him. As the vizier of the god-king Amenhotep, he facilitated many of the numerous roles the ruler was required to assume. That very morning, Amenemopet had met with a number of overseers who were in charge of various aspects of Egypt's well-being. The reports were, as predictable, professional and mostly positive: the granaries were sufficient to handle any crisis, and tribute from the 'pacified' territories continued to be delivered. There were also updates on building projects including the ruler's own memorial temple and the construction of his royal tomb.

Amenemopet felt hugely honoured to be serving his childhood friend, and his duties were varied and often interesting. His favourite days were the parades of tribute from subdued lands from the south and east and he enjoyed meeting their emissaries, who spread baskets of precious shiny things at his feet if the ruler wasn't present. Unfortunately, mundane reports from across the realm were the usual case, more often than not, but being as close as one could be to administrating the general affairs of Egypt, he shouldn't complain.

Being so close to the ruler was both a benefit and a curse. Every meal was the best that Egypt had to offer, and Amenemopet took full advantage. Tall and very heavy, his aches and pains were beginning to accumulate and being out of breath was now somewhat the norm. Hiking up to his own tomb demonstrated to the vizier himself that he was tired and under-exercised, but with the help of a tall staff and short rests he was capable of making the journey.

On this day, Amenemopet was accompanied by the young scribe Dagi, who was recommended by a senior palace scribe as an up-and-coming fellow worthy of mentorship. Dagi walked several steps behind the vizier, carrying his writing kit, some paper for taking notes, and a net bag with some bread and a small flask of water. The scribe had never been to Thebes's west bank, the cemetery of Egypt's elites, but thus far it was turning out to be an intriguing journey, with the river crossed on a luxury boat and a ride in a chariot beside the mighty vizier.

'So what exactly are we doing here today, O Vizier?' asked Dagi naively.

'We are here to check on the status of my own tomb, which I've neglected for some time,' explained Amenemopet. 'And you will take notes as needed, or otherwise assist me.'

The trail wound among dozens of prestigious tombs carved into the hillsides, some with expansive courtyards and impressive white vertical façades. It was easy to identify their owners; inscribed door jambs and lintels celebrated the deceased, and a peek into their impressive funerary chapels revealed painted walls with glorifying biographies, and illustrations of lavish offerings to the deceased, elaborate funerals, and views of an ideal Afterlife.

Before inspecting the progress of his own tomb, Amenemopet paused to examine a couple of tomb chapels belonging to two individuals who had played important roles in his life. Each chapel was a tribute to its owner and would hopefully be visited by family and friends on feast days or other special occasions. The first was that of his occupational predecessor, the vizier Rekhmire. Over the course of his long career, he had held thirty titles other than vizier, and first served ably under the rule of Thutmose III and thereafter with Amenhotep, before passing away. He had been overseer of the gold and silver treasuries, the archives and the construction works of Amun. And he had served as a priest and a judge, along with a variety of other important positions inside the palace and elsewhere. In contrast, Amenemopet had thus far acquired only nine titles, but his role as vizier was the ultimate administrative position attainable for a non-royal in Egypt. Having attended the funeral, Amenemopet was well aware that somewhere in the vicinity was a deep buried shaft in which the body of the old vizier lay in his coffin in an adjacent small chamber crowded with burial goods. Perhaps they were standing directly atop him.

The two visitors entered the chapel, which consisted of a major hall directly ahead and two corridors to the left and right. The plastered and painted walls were stunning, illustrating a variety of activities including the vizier inspecting exotic tribute from distant lands, and effectively carrying out other duties. There were depictions of some of his family members and wonderful scenes of craftsmen producing all manner of glamorous goods including jewellery and furniture, scenes that would transform into spiritual reality for the deceased.

'Take note,' ordered the vizier to his scribe. 'I would like something similar. And an impressive summary of my numerous accomplishments is expected.'

'His funeral must have been exceptional,' commented the young scribe.

'Indeed it was,' responded Amenemopet. 'Although it wasn't much different from the burial of a very wealthy man, it was quite the entourage with Amenhotep himself in attendance, and the highest officials of the land. The procession of superb grave goods was impressive with furniture, food, wine and linen all carried up the path by strong men, followed by dozens of wailing women. The coffin eventually arrived, of course, as did the jars containing his entrails.'

**The funeral of a wealthy Egyptian. Priests perform the Opening of the Mouth ceremony in front of the deceased's tomb while mourners show their grief**

The vizier went on to give a brief description of what followed. Rekhmire's coffin was set standing upright and a lector priest began to read the proper liturgy. Another specialized priest with a leopard skin over his shoulder performed the Opening of the Mouth ceremony, in which he touched the lips of the coffin lid's face with an adze to ensure that the deceased's voice could once again speak. A freshly amputated cow's leg and the bovine's heart were also held up to the coffin to further enhance Rekhmire's reanimation. As the vizier's coffin and grave goods were lowered down a shaft into a simple chamber, a grand banquet began in the courtyard for the distinguished guests. 'It was one of the best parties I've ever attended,' commented Amenemopet, 'and that cow's leg didn't go to waste! We cooked it right there!'

Not far away was the tomb of Amenemopet's own brother Sennefer, who performed well over twenty different roles during his career, including serving as the mayor of the city of Thebes. His chapel, too, was beautifully decorated. Although more or less on the same plan as that of Rekhmire's, the main hall of Sennefer's tomb ended in a chamber with four pillars. There were scenes of offerings by the deceased to the gods, many offerings to the deceased himself, representations of family members, and depictions of an idyllic eternal existence. Amenemopet had watched with his brother the construction of the tomb and hoped to match its quality with his own nearby.

The vizier knew a secret only known by very few, not even by most of those who attended Sennefer's funeral. Sennefer was neither buried in a shaft in the courtyard nor one in the floor of the chapel. Beneath the chapel itself was a magnificent pillared chamber with lavish painted decorations. With its ceiling irregular due to the quality of rock, the artists had painted bunches of grapes, thus adding a delightful and unique, if not realistic, touch to the room. Sennefer and his accompanying grave goods lay within, the chamber's entrance buried and obscured, his resting place a unique and desirable place.

With an increasing feeling of anxiety, Amenemopet led Dagi to his own neighbouring and unfinished tomb. At first sight, the vizier felt somewhat embarrassed at its progress. With so many professional duties to attend to, and some annoyances with the expenses involved, the chapel remained unfinished. Still, it was respectable, with its entrance leading into a chamber with four and a half pillars, so far, from which a rectangular hall extended. 'It's not bad,' commented the vizier, 'but it still requires a lot of

## A CEMETERY FOR THE ELITE OF THEBES

The tombs of Rekhmire and Sennefer are just two of the hundreds of tombs of ancient officials built into the foothills on the west bank of the river in Thebes. The cemetery, known today as the 'Theban necropolis' or the 'Tombs of the Nobles' is famous for its beautifully decorated tomb chapels whose texts and paintings have provided a vital source of information about specific individuals, historical events, funerary beliefs, and life in ancient Egypt in general. Several centuries ago, a village called 'Gurna' was established among the tombs, with the inhabitants often incorporating the chambers of various tombs into their homes. With the increase of foreign tourists in the nineteenth century, some of the villagers began excavating under their homes to recover antiquities to sell. In 2009, Gurna was evacuated and then bulldozed to protect the tombs, and its residents were relocated to a more modern settlement nearby.

work. I need to sit down.' Amenemopet found a random stone block lying in the tomb's mostly finished courtyard. Coughing, gasping and wheezing, he wondered how much longer he might live. After a few minutes enjoying the fresh air, Dagi helped the vizier to his feet and assisted him back to where the chariot and horses awaited.

Amenemopet harboured another secret that few knew. As he was the very dear friend of the ruler, Amenhotep had granted him an incredible privilege: the vizier would be allowed to be buried in the royal cemetery in a very simple undecorated tomb close to his own. Amenemopet's chapel in the Theban foothills would remain for those who might care to visit, but his mummified body in its coffin, and a small selection of grave goods, would be interred in a small single-chamber at the bottom of a shaft close to the grandiose tomb of Amenhotep himself. There was no greater honour imaginable.

## THE FARMER AND THE FISHERMEN

For weeks, Baki had watched the Nile slowly subside, and it wouldn't be long before the next stage of the agricultural cycle would begin. The fields had to be prepared and the irrigation ditches dug out and made ready. As expected, the Nile's gift of rich black slime blanketed the landscape, ensuring that the soil would be fertile and the crops abundant, provided that proper planting, maintenance and harvesting were performed.

Leaving his home with a basket in one hand and a hoe over his shoulder, Baki walked down to the field, dreading the task of locating and scooping muck out of old irrigation ditches. Mutui knew that his efforts would result in her husband returning tired and muddy.

Sometimes there were issues regarding property boundaries after the flood. An unscrupulous neighbour could move a stone marker to his slight advantage and perhaps even claim that the original marker had been washed away in the flood. It was a matter not to be taken lightly and there could be heavy consequences should the perpetrator be found guilty. But this year, at least, Baki found all was in order.

Downstream, Nefer, Weni and the other fishermen were enjoying some easy fishing. With the water in retreat, a few pools could be found here and there, in which catfish and other fish had become trapped. Some of the fish were huge and could be easily netted or speared. 'O Nefer! We're as skilled as Thanuny!' laughed Weni as he speared an immense catfish, which violently wriggled on the end of his harpoon. Unfortunately, as had happened several times that day, the catfish managed to flop itself into the river proper and swim away before it could be subdued.

Nefer put his club down and grabbed one of his favourite tools: a triangular tapered net with its mouth reinforced with wooden staves. It was great for catching smaller trapped fish, which could be readily scooped out of the temporary pools. A good sweep would cause a great splashing and sometimes half a dozen would end up in the net. The day's catch was impressive and Weni began to congratulate himself as he grabbed several more baskets to fill. 'Don't be so impressed with yourself,' admonished Nefer, 'those pools will be dried up in just a few days and then we are back in the skiffs!'

After quickly gutting and cleaning dozens of fish, Nefer grabbed some twine and ran it through their gills, while some of the huge catfish were impaled in the same manner but on a thin pole for easy carrying between two men.

'Your uncle will be so impressed!' exclaimed Weni.

'Don't be so naïve,' replied Nefer. 'He will still grumble no matter how many fish we provide. Let's keep the biggest one for ourselves. He'll never know.'

# Second Month of the Season of Sowing and Growing

## THE PHYSICIAN

It was early afternoon when the frantic woman appeared at the door of the one-room village clinic, holding a small screaming boy in her arms. The youngster had been playing in an acacia tree and slipped, impaling his right forearm on a long slender branch, which snapped off on impact. The physician, Neferhotep, placed the child on the floor and held down the wriggling body while his son, Nakht, approached the patient with a small bronze saw. The sight of the sharp implement increased the boy's panic but it was only to be used to saw off the stick close to skin level before removing what was left. That accomplished, a pair of metal tweezers was produced and with a quick but skilled jerk, a long sliver of wood was expertly extracted from the patient's limb.

Nakht then massaged the now-bleeding arm to help ensure there was nothing left inside before applying pressure to the wound. With the most painful part of the procedure over, the boy calmed down a bit while his mother and the two physicians offered kind and reassuring words. After a few minutes, Nakht checked to see that the bleeding had stopped and grabbed a nearby jar of honey. Dipping his fingers within, he vigorously rubbed the substance in and around the small hole and then wound a linen bandage several times around the skinny limb. 'Do what I just did with some honey every day, and bring him back to me if he develops an illness,' he instructed the mother. 'And here,' Nakht continued as he reached into a wooden box. 'Put this amulet around his neck; it should help with his healing.' The small object was made of blue faience and represented a healing god, Thoth. Neferhotep let go of the boy and brought him to his feet. 'Pay us later,' he suggested as he escorted the two to the door of the clinic. 'And keep him out of the acacia trees!'

Neferhotep was impressed with his son's work and told him so. The boy had learned from the best. Neferhotep had spent years in this very room, lined as it was with small jars, boxes and a pile of scrolls stacked up in a corner. Situated at Thebes, near the river and close to several major building projects, he had treated, most more successfully than not, an incredible variety of injuries, from simple skin rashes to patients crushed by stone blocks. There were lots of cuts, broken bones, abdominal pains, crocodile and hippo bites, cloudy eyes, pregnancy issues, heart maladies, and even the occasional repeat customers who exhibited no signs or illness, along with some who requested non-essential cures for baldness or the like. Neferhotep learned never to be surprised and there was usually some sort of healing that could be attempted whether it involved surgery, purges, poultices or medicants to be inserted in various body cavities. The scrolls offered advice on symptoms and suggested cures, but equally importantly, carried the texts of incantations to deities to aid in the healing process. Magic was a part of the process and the gods could be further honoured and invoked by amulets, boxes of which were kept close at hand.

THE OPENING PAGE OF THE EBERS PAPYRUS, A MEDICAL TEXT FROM
THE NEW KINGDOM, ADDRESSING A VARIETY OF MALADIES

Neferhotep had been a physician now for about twenty years and was the son of a physician, as were his father and grandfather, following numerous preceding generations in the same profession. Nakht was his only son, his mother having died while giving birth, a situation not uncommon, despite the attention of experienced midwives. Neferhotep had been tending to a patient and by the time he arrived home, his wife was no longer alive. Although an incredibly sad situation, it was always a possibility, and dead patients were often brought to the clinic in desperate attempts to save those beyond help. 'We will see her in the beautiful Afterlife,' he often assured his son who began his education in scribal school.

After his lessons every day, young Nakht would rush home to help his father in the clinic. Although often reprimanded for causing distractions or making inappropriate comments about the patients, he was allowed to assist with treatments and even diagnose various maladies as he matured. And after learning to effectively read and write, he spent time studying his father's medical scrolls and those housed in the Per-Ankh, the House of Life, a medical school library located in a nearby temple. Now twenty-four years old, Nakht was mostly on his own. Neferhotep was only in Thebes at this time for a short visit to attend the wedding of his niece, a raucous affair that resulted in him being asked for assistance after a few minor trips and falls on the part of drunken guests. And with knowledge that a skilled physician was in the house, Neferhotep was constantly badgered by attendees who unashamedly requested quick looks at rashes on various parts of their bodies or bald spots. As everyone knew, Neferhotep was no longer an ordinary village physician; he was presently the Chief Royal Physician, tending to none other than the ruler, Amenhotep himself, along with his family and closest associates.

## A Chariot Accident

Although Neferhotep possessed an outstanding reputation as one of the better physicians in the Theban region, it was a chance encounter with one of the ruler's closest friends, Ptahemhat, that would initiate his elevation to higher office. The physician remembered the incident exceedingly well. Like Amenhotep himself, Ptahemhat was a sporting fellow, and occasionally enjoyed engaging in risky activities. A few years previously, Neferhotep was walking not far from his home when he heard a joyous cry and the sound of racing hooves on a dry road at the edge of the green fields where the agriculture ends and the desert begins. A man dressed in fine linen clothes stood in the back of a chariot pulled by a pair of horses seemingly being driven to run their fastest. 'What a fool,' concluded Neferhotep. More than once he had seen the consequences of this sort of thing and it was usually a top military official or someone else associated with the palace. Although the ruler had a legendary reputation for the same sort of antics, he seemed to have slowed down considerably in the last several years.

## CHARIOTS

Pharaohs fighting in chariots drawn by rearing horses is a well-known motif on some New Kingdom royal monuments. The chariots, though, were a relatively late addition to the Egyptian war machine, appearing just before Egypt's age of empire when the technology was introduced from foreign lands to the east. Apart from their use in battle, often as an effective platform for archers, chariots also served as grand domestic vehicles for the ruler and other elites. Six complete and well-preserved chariots were found within the tomb of Tutankhamun and have provided a wealth of information on their construction and use.

Within moments, the anticipated loud crash was heard. One of the spokes in the chariot's two wooden wheels had snapped causing the vehicle to collapse and buckle with its occupant being dragged underneath. The horses sensed as much and came to a slow halt, twisting and neighing in agitation as Neferhotep dashed to the scene. Expecting to find the charioteer contorted and dead, the physician instead found the man gasping for air having been pinned beneath the vehicle's frame. With great effort, he was able to pull back an obstructing panel, allowing the injured man to regain breaths of fresh air.

The charioteer moaned as Neferhotep pulled him out of the wreckage and it was clear that this was a nobleman. Only later would he learn his identity: the well-known and esteemed royal confidant, Ptahemhat, childhood friend and fan-bearer of Amenhotep. The physician gave him a quick examination, listening to his breathing, feeling his pulses, checking for dents in his head and observing the numerous swellings and expected scrapes. Working his way down the victim's body, Neferhotep pulled up the driver's linen skirt to reveal what appeared to be his only severe injury, evidenced by a bulge in his upper left leg. It was clearly broken and nearly in two, but fortunately hadn't penetrated through the skin.

By that time, several farmers and others from the nearby village had gathered around the spectacle and Neferhotep ordered four men to gently pick up the profoundly confused patient and bring him to the clinic. Once there, using great care, a now-moaning Ptahemhat was laid on his back on a bed of folded linen with a bundle of the same material placed under his head as a pillow. Asking all to step outside, except for Nakht who was in attendance, Neferhotep repeated his exam and upon reaching the injured leg, felt it with his fingertips for several minutes. 'I think we can help,' he informed his son. 'Let's give him a few sips of water and if he drinks it well, give him a cup of date wine. Mix it with some mandrake powder and we'll put him to sleep. And place a few amulets around his neck.' Nakht knew what would come next. After a few minutes of the wine concoction taking effect, his father would attempt to realign the two halves of the snapped bone into their proper orientation.

A broken upper leg was always difficult, there usually being a lot of thick flesh in the way. Neferhotep had attempted it numerous times before and there were several grateful people in the Theban area who had survived the procedure well enough to continue life more or less as normal. Fortunately, in this case, Ptahemhat's leg appeared to be rather thin and unexercised, thus increasing the prospect of success.

## MEDICAL PRESCRIPTIONS

Egyptian medicine made use of a great variety of substances – animal, vegetable and mineral – which on their own or when combined were used in an attempt to produce the desired results. A few ancient medical texts, mostly written on papyrus, have survived and allow us a glimpse of treatments for conditions ranging from life-threatening traumatic injuries to cures for baldness. Some of the more interesting ingredients include donkey milk, an old book cooked in oil, dust of a statue, the film of dampness found on the wood of ships, crushed hog's tooth, blood of a vulture, head of an eel and cat dung. One recipe for curing baldness involves a mixture in equal portions of fat from a hippo, crocodile, lion, snake, cat and ibex, to be rubbed into the scalp.

With the victim's body arranged in the best possible alignment, the procedure began. 'Ready, Nakht?' asked Neferhotep as he felt for the edges of the bone through Ptahemhat's skin. 'Now tug on his knee while I pull and twist.' The patient let out a huge huff. The procedure took only a few seconds as the injured man's leg was expertly realigned, but the swelling in the area of the injury was considerable as expected. 'Let's clean him up,' ordered Neferhotep as the two gently pulled away Ptahemhat's ripped clothing and carefully washed every scrape and cut. Nakht was left to apply honey and bandages to all, while his father prepared a poultice composed of alum, cow's milk mixed with barley, and clay that would be bound to the area of the break with rigid wooden splints on each side.

With the treatment now nearly completed, the work of the two physicians was interrupted when two stern, elegantly dressed officials entered the room. 'Is he alive?' one asked.

'Yes, although perhaps he shouldn't be,' answered the physician. 'He had quite a crash and was dying when we found him. He has a fractured leg but we reset and bound it. He's just resting now.'

'Do you know who this is?' asked the other official.

'We don't,' responded Neferhotep, 'but given his clothes and the fact that he was driving a very expensive chariot, I would conclude that he's quite an important man.'

'He is. This is Ptahemhat, fan-bearer of Aakheperure Amenhotep. The ruler himself allowed him to borrow the vehicle and horses, but perhaps he should slow down. I smell date wine. Was he drunk when you found him?'

'Not at all,' answered Neferhotep. 'We gave him wine to dull the pain when we treated him.'

'We are taking him back to the palace. We have our own excellent physicians that can tend to him there.'

The two men disappeared and returned with a donkey harnessed to a cart cushioned with layers of cloth, commandeered from a farmer, along with several strong men who lifted Ptahemhat into the cart. Without further words, the reckless fan-bearer was driven away in the direction of the ruler's Theban home.

## The Physician is Promoted

The following few months thereafter had been business as usual with the expected parade of patients with both minor and consequential afflictions. The chariot incident was quickly becoming just another memory when one of the palace officials who took away Ptahemhat arrived with an order: 'Your presence is requested at the palace. Replace those disgusting filthy clothes with your best and meet me outside.' Neferhotep took no offence. It was true, the medical profession could leave one bloodied or otherwise soiled at the end of a busy day. He did as told and the two walked down to the river, where a small, beautifully appointed boat awaited, complete with four oarsmen as crew. The official offered no explanation and his abrupt manner was disconcerting. Had Ptahemhat died as a result of his treatment? Neferhotep would soon find out. Reaching the pier near the palace grounds, the two disembarked and walked through the impressive gates to the royal residence.

The guards quickly ushered them into a courtyard where Neferhotep was turned over to another man who introduced himself as 'Inspector of Palace Physicians'. 'Come with me,' he commanded and the two walked down several corridors to a well-lit room simply outfitted with a bed and a chair, the former occupied by a still body, lying on its back, a wooden pillow supporting his head. 'Could this be the charioteer and he's dead?' thought Neferhotep.

Hearing the two enter the room, the body sat up and offered a wide grin. It was indeed Ptahemhat, who then rotated to the edge of the bed, grabbed a long staff from against the wall and pulled himself to his feet with his arms. Approaching Neferhotep with careful steps, the former patient greeted him with a long embrace. 'Your treatment with the gods' help has healed me. I have a gift for you. I have spoken with the ruler, and have asked that you become a physician of the palace. He agreed and the inspector here also agreed that your efforts were excellent. As you know, we are sometimes here and often in Memphis and this is a great honour. I hope you will accept!'

Neferhotep had been overwhelmed with the offer and after a fine meal with Ptahemhat and the inspector, he informed them both that he would let them know of his decision in the coming days. Yes, it was a great honour and a real change of pace from the daily blood and grime of a village physician's work, but a discussion with his son was important. Nakht was both thrilled and intimidated by the news; thrilled for his father, but intimidated by the reality that he would now be operating the clinic by himself, a daunting but inevitable outcome for the young physician. But how could his father turn down such an opportunity! Neferhotep agreed and promised that if based at the palace in Memphis, he would travel to Thebes as often as he could find an excuse.

Neferhotep's first experience as a palace physician had been a somewhat nerve-wracking prospect. He was in impressive company with well-experienced colleagues, some who had worked in the palace for decades. They were a remarkable collection of Egypt's best experts in everything that might possibly afflict the members of the royal family and its household, including specialists in specific body parts, and even teeth. Most had heard the tale of the rescue of Ptahemhat, with some being impressed, and others appearing a bit resentful at Neferhotep's quick promotion. Still, there was no doubting his qualifications and the variety and depth of his experience. All of the inspectors of the palace physicians were impressed by his knowledge, and any scepticism soon turned to respect.

Meeting the ruler for the first time had been frightening. Neferhotep had seen him a few times from a distance during some of the Theban festivals, but never close-up and in-person. 'He might have the body of a man, but never forget that he still is a god,' he was often warned. On the appointed day, Neferhotep, dressed in fine white linen, was led through the Memphis palace to what he could only assume was the royal chamber of meeting. There were several people milling about, all impressively clothed, including Ptahemhat, who slowly

A RELIEF IN THE TOMB AT GIZA OF THE FIRST INTERMEDIATE
PERIOD ROYAL PHYSICIAN, IRENAKHTY, NOTES SOME OF
HIS AREAS OF EXPERTISE INCLUDING OPHTHALMOLOGY,
GASTROENTEROLOGY AND PROCTOLOGY

walked forward unassisted to illustrate the success of
his healing.

'Come, Neferhotep!' exclaimed the fan-bearer.

The physician followed Ptahemhat over to where a
small group of men were convened in conversation. Seeing
the two approaching they parted, and Neferhotep nearly
fainted. There, seated in a stunning gilded chair was the
ruler himself, Aakheperure Amenhotep. He looked a lot

older and more frail than the carved stone likenesses he had seen here and there, and his hair was greying with a bald spot. The physician fell to his knees and kissed the plastered floor while Amenhotep chuckled. 'Get up! You must be the one who helped my friend Ptahemhat, during his chariot antics. Good work. You'll be happy to know that I've advised him to no longer drink wine prior to borrowing my chariots.'

'He wasn't drunk,' stuttered Neferhotep nervously, embarrassed that his first words to the living god were, 'He wasn't drunk.' Both Amenhotep and Ptahemhat laughed and the physician was set at ease.

'You need not fear me,' the ruler assured. 'After all, you will be examining and helping myself, my family, and many others among the most important people in Egypt.'

## THE RULER BECOMES ILL

It quickly became clear that there was a friendly chemistry between Amenhotep and Neferhotep, and the new royal physician was increasingly called first when there was a matter of general concern. Within two years, he had been promoted to the position of Inspector of the Palace Physicians, an important role that he took very seriously in ensuring the high quality of care constantly required. Due to his growing popularity with Amenhotep and the royal family, Neferhotep quickly rose to the rank of Chief Royal Physician when the previous holder of the office unexpectedly died after a short illness. It was an envied elevation, but after years treating a constant stream of ailments in Thebes, he felt both competent and honoured.

This particular day, Nakht closed the clinic after the boy with the stick through his arm was treated. Neferhotep had left Memphis with the ruler in the competent hands of a dozen or so medical experts, and with the wedding of his niece over, it was time for him to return to his post in Memphis. At the dock adjacent to the Theban palace, he boarded a small official boat travelling north, and with a good steersman, it would take only about a week to reach his destination. It was a relaxing voyage with beautiful scenery on each side worth savouring while he could, and the cabin on board provided shade and a comfortable place to sleep.

Just a few hours before reaching Memphis, however, another royal vessel was seen heading directly for them, its sail aloft and almost on a collision course. The two boats pulled next to each other and Neferhotep recognized the captain, Ipu, who ordered him to change ships as his presence was required immediately at the palace on the orders of Tiaa, Amenhotep's queen. The exchange took place quickly, and Ipu ordered a dozen men to lower the sail and put oars in the water to return to the port of Memphis. The captain insisted that he wasn't aware of the details, but obviously it was a matter of extreme importance, and Neferhotep could only speculate with great anxiety.

Reaching Memphis, Ipu escorted the physician to an awaiting chariot and driver that would bring him swiftly to the palace in a matter of minutes. All remained curiously silent as he was ushered through the gates and into a room where he could thoroughly wash his body before changing into fresh clean linens that were provided. Now prepared for what might lie ahead, Neferhotep was led quickly by a servant to Amenhotep's dimly lit private sleeping quarters and was shocked at what he encountered. Lying on the ornate royal bed was the ruler himself, drenched in sweat and delirious. Tiaa was prone on the floor crying while Ptahemhat, gently weeping, waved a cooling fan over his master and friend. On each end of the bed were gilded statues of Isis and Thoth, and on Amenhotep's wet chest were laid several amulets of gold and precious stones, probably placed there by the pair of priestesses of Sekhmet chanting nearby. Several of the palace physicians stepped aside when Neferhotep approached and he was well aware that each had thus far done their best. Upon questioning, they described how over the past week, the ruler had complained of a pain in his lower right abdomen that grew more intense each day. Concluding that he was suffering from an abundance of rotting waste within his body, they injected medicinal enemas, rubbed concoctions on his abdomen, and provided him with drinks that would provoke vomiting. Each treatment produced some results, but Amenhotep was soon vomiting without provocation, and was completely incapacitated, growing more ill with the passing of each hour.

Neferhotep approached Amenhotep, putting his ear up to the ruler's open mouth. It was clear that he was still breathing although quite shallowly. Next, the physician felt the patient's pulse in several areas of the body starting

## EGYPTIAN LIFE SPAN

There were hundreds of ways to die in ancient Egypt. Infections from injuries were common and bites from animals such as crocodiles, snakes and hippos, and scorpion stings, could have dire consequences. One could drown in the Nile or fall victim to an 'industrial accident' at one of Egypt's many construction projects. Childbirth, too, could be a very hazardous experience. Examinations of mummies have shown that diseases such as bilharzia, tuberculosis and malaria were not uncommon. It's possible, too, that plagues might have occasionally taken their toll, and participation in the military had its own set of dangers. An ancient Egyptian might expect to live only thirty to thirty-five years, but some attained great age, including the powerful New Kingdom pharaoh Rameses II, who ruled for sixty-seven years and might have lived to about age ninety.

at the neck, and then listened to the fading thumps of his heart. Pressing and feeling with expert fingers, Neferhotep examined every inch of the royal body, noting great warmth emanating from the area reported by his colleagues. The Chief Royal Physician once more questioned his colleagues about their treatment but could find nothing amiss or lacking. Neferhotep again approached the nearly lifeless body of Amenhotep and began to recite an incantation that he had memorized from his youth:

> *I have come with the Great One of the Great House, the Lords of Protection and the Rulers of Eternity, and with the Mother of the Gods. They have given you their protection. I have utterances that the Lord of the Universe has composed to eliminate the doings of a god, a goddess, a dead man, a dead woman . . . that are in your head, in your vertebrae, in this your shoulders, in these your flesh and limbs.*

And with the best that the best could do, all that could be done was to wait for what seemed inevitable, with hopes that the gods would intervene and cure one of their own. Peering into the room from the doorway was the young prince Thutmose, his face emotionless and his future in question. The next few hours or days would be decisive.

## THE FARMER AND HERDSMAN COLLABORATE

Over the last few weeks, the black slime deposits had dried out sufficiently to allow ploughing and planting. It was actually something Baki looked forward to, and the process was facilitated with the occasional help of both Mutui and his best friend, Senna the herdsman. In return for his assistance, the latter would receive a few baskets of grain at the end of the year, and the assurance that Baki would in turn assist him if ever needed.

When the time came to sow, Senna appeared with a couple of 'borrowed' sturdy cattle to which Baki hitched a large wooden hoe with handles. As the farmer managed the churning up of the soil by controlling the plough and applying weight to its share, the herdsman led the bovines along a prescribed course. Although her work was mostly confined to her many domestic duties, Mutui assisted in the fields for several days each year by walking in front of the cattle and spreading seed to be trampled and hoed into the ground. It was a lot of work but the effort was lightened as jokes were told and songs were sung. Life was excellent, at the moment at least. The sun shone bright, the birds chirped, and the majestic river flowed on. It was a beautiful day for the team in the field, blissfully unaware of the profound drama unfolding up north in Memphis.

**PLOUGHING AND SOWING AN EGYPTIAN FIELD**

# Third Month of the Season of Sowing and Growing

## THE RULER DIES

It had only been a couple of days since Amenhotep had fallen ill, and he had been unresponsive to all attempts at treatment. Tiaa lay on a mat not far from his bed, while another rotation of priestesses of Sekhmet continued to chant, their shadows flickering on the walls in the dimly lit chamber. The Chief Royal Physician, Neferhotep, managed to catch a few moments of rest on occasion but was regularly awakened to discuss an untried possible cure or the suggestion that another specific demon was at work. There had already been many attempts at exorcism by identifying and calling out the name of a suspected malevolent spirit, but with little effect. Ptahemhat remained distraught, his arms weary from fanning the ruler, who began to sweat less and less, a sign interpreted by some of the physicians as improvement, but Neferhotep was less optimistic. His regular checks of breath and pulse portended a dwindling of life.

Around midnight on the fourth day of the ruler's failing health, Neferhotep examined the still, prone body yet again. The prognosis was clear: Aakheperure Amenhotep was dead. Neferhotep was cautious and wanted to be absolutely sure, checking the patient several more times while contemplating how he would make the announcement to others in the room. Rising from his knees from the end of the bed, he spread out his arms and gave a nod to the priestesses and fan-bearers. With the cessation of all sound, Tiaa looked up, anticipating the dreaded statement. Slowly and deliberately, Neferhotep uttered a rare phrase that would soon ring throughout the land, a dramatic if not traumatic statement well remembered from more than two decades prior with the death of Thutmose III: 'the falcon has risen into heaven.'

The sobbing was almost instantaneous and unanimous, with tears even welling up in the eyes of the typically stoic royal physicians. Tiaa let out a high-pitched shriek, arising from the floor to fling herself on the body of her husband while the priestesses began to wail. The vizier, Amenemopet, approached the head guard at the door. 'Tell no one! Soon, all in Egypt will know but not yet.' There was reason for abundant caution: the ruler's greater role was to maintain *maat*: cosmic truth and order, and to keep chaos at bay. With his death, turmoil was a possibility. The universe was now poised on the tip of a balance, and the forces of evil could emerge to destabilize the Two Lands. It was a situation to be taken with the utmost seriousness and given the possibility of panic among the populace, the announcement would need to be made with consideration and discretion.

Prince Thutmose stepped forward to comfort his mother. Sad but stone-faced, he placed his hand on her shoulder and soberly stood by. Neferhotep approached the other physicians to discuss the next steps. 'We'll leave his majesty here for a few hours and then the embalmers will remove him. This will give us some time for the present company to express their grief as preparations are made.' After the first day of vigorous treatment, Neferhotep had privately predicted the outcome, and had quietly asked that embalming equipment and related materials of the utmost quality be discreetly transported and delivered, with the identity of the deceased not revealed. A special tent had been erected within the palace compound where the mummification would take place.

In a land where secrets are difficult to keep, rumours had already been flying that someone of great importance was dying. Could it be one of the princes or the queen herself, or one of the cherished friends of the ruler? It certainly couldn't be Aakheperure Amenhotep, the perfect athlete and embodiment of health! Prince Thutmose, who appeared somewhat delicate and pampered, was a favourite candidate to be the deceased, but soon, the fact that the ruler was dead became the consensus, and the word from there quickly spread throughout Memphis and rapidly proliferated in all directions.

In the remarkable ways that traumatic news can travel far faster than through normal means, the death of Amenhotep and its accompanying sadness and fear would soon reach Thebes and beyond. As might be expected, speculation over his cause of death was rampant and went well beyond the actual medical situation. Had he been murdered? Was there a usurper in the palace? Was it an accident while engaging in some sort of hunting or other sport? Did he drown while hunting hippos – a representation of chaos – in a papyrus swamp?

## THE EMBALMERS

Under the supervision of Mahu, the most respected embalmer in Memphis, everything was prepared in the tent, and his assistants waited for orders from the vizier to fetch the body. Mummifying royalty was a rare event. The last had taken place just a few years previously when this same team had embalmed Prince Webensenu with utmost care, his coffined body placed in a side chamber of the ruler's own royal tomb in the Theban mountains. Amenhotep would be treated with the supreme respect. There would be no joking around as might have been the case in embalming facilities for those of lesser status. There would be no ridicule of big noses, large feet or tiny body parts. This was no mere mortal, but a god-king.

Mahu had learned his trade beginning in his youth. He started out in a provincial embalming facility maintaining incense and light, and then progressed to washing tools and fetching natron and linen. Eventually, he was allowed to deal with some of the bodies themselves, moving them where necessary, catching entrails in bowls, and rubbing down corpses with oil. Given more responsibilities over the many years, his skill with both the low- and high-end mummification processes became recognized, and he began to be requested for the preparation of some of the most elite of deceased.

After several hours, Amenemopet gave the word, and a litter was brought into the chamber to remove Amenhotep. Those surrounding his body continued to cry but stepped aside as Mahu gently placed a linen sheet over the corpse and then supervised the lifting from the bed to the litter. With the utmost of respect, four members of the embalming team slowly and sombrely carried the litter away on a circuitous path to their tent where all was ready.

Like so many Egyptians, Mahu had only seen the ruler from a distance. His first view of Amenhotep's inanimate body was both startling and awe-inspiring, and even with his great experience, the incredible responsibility of embalming a god-king was intimidating. There were few in his profession who ever had the honour, and the last was twenty-six years ago when the third Thutmose likewise flew to heaven. Mahu could see that his assistants were terrified and shaking as they carried the litter through the palace to the awaiting tent. Guards at the entrance pulled back the door flap and the cortege proceeded inside.

The embalming tent was indeed well prepared. There were jars containing some of the most expensive and purest of oils, stacks of the finest linen, trays bearing a variety of metal tools, and most importantly, large pots containing perhaps the most essential ingredient of them all, natron. This white, fine-grained substance was found in the desert to the north-west of Memphis. Its property as a desiccant had been known for millennia and if one were to preserve a body for the ages, it would need to be dried out. Caravans of donkeys regularly made the trip to collect large quantities of natron to service the busy embalming business all over Egypt.

## MUMMIFICATION INGREDIENTS

Natron, the desiccating agent used in mummification, is a natural substance found within ancient dry lake beds most prominently in the Wadi Natroun located in Egypt's Western Desert. Among its chemical components are sodium carbonate, sodium bicarbonate and salt. Bags and jars of soiled or fresh natron are occasionally found in tombs, or in caches containing embalming supplies. Other ingredients sometimes used in the mummification process included imported frankincense and myrrh, tree resins from pines and firs, and beeswax.

It was important for the body to bear a resemblance to its once-living owner. That way, it would remain recognizable to its soul, or *ka*, which would hopefully survive and thrive despite the mortality of the deceased, being sustained by all of the offerings recorded on a tomb owner's chapel walls and the actual provisions interred with the body. Sadly, not everyone could afford the treatment, nor an elaborate coffin and grave goods; in fact, the majority of Egyptians could not. Mahu was a compassionate fellow, and he was saddened that the average villager, whose work sustained the Two Lands, would likely be buried in a simple hole in the ground at the desert's edge. A few jugs of beer, a necklace of faience amulets, and perhaps even a hair comb might be all that could be provided.

On the other hand, those with a few more resources available had several options, including basic evisceration and drying, a cursory but respectable wrapping in cheap linen bandages, and placement in a simple undecorated coffin. From there, the expenses could grow significantly with the quality of materials used, and the amount of time and care provided to produce a fine mummy. A cheap process might result in something passable, but perhaps resembling more a salted fish than a once-breathing human being, while the ultimate process, such as the one about to take place, would hopefully produce something more resembling the deceased merely taking a nap.

Mahu was well aware that timing was important. The processes that cause a body to decay begin rapidly after death and there was little time to waste if one was to produce the best possible outcome. Pulling the linen sheet off Amenhotep, Mahu got his first real look at his project. Pale and emaciated, mouth agape and eyes wide open, he bore no resemblance to the honed athletic hero he had been raised to admire. The embalming assistants seemed paralysed with fear, each taking a cautious look. 'We have important work to do, let's get started,' ordered their boss. One of the embalmers fetched a few jars of pleasant-smelling juniper oil and stacks of clean linen of the highest quality, while an apprentice was charged with keeping the lamps lit and the incense fresh. Amenhotep was then gently lifted on to a low, thin stone slab, its edges creased with channels to capture fluids draining away from the body.

The first step was to completely clean the body, washing it perfectly, and then rubbing preservative oils into the flesh. The next stage was crucial and the most exacting: the removal of most of the internal organs and the brain. With the cleaned body on its back, Mahu selected an incredibly sharp obsidian blade from a tray held by an assistant. Another aide knelt down with several large bowls, each partially filled with the purest of natron. With solemn reverance, the embalmer pulled the knife's blade across the lower left side of Amenhotep's abdomen, making a few practice swipes before cutting a deep diagonal slit.

With confidence born of years of experience, Mahu thrust his hand into the gash and began to pull out masses of glistening intestines, all being deposited into one of the bowls. A knife was applied to disconnect anything connecting one internal bit with another. The bowl was immediately taken away to have jars of natron copiously

## BELIEFS ABOUT THE BRAIN

Although physicians acknowledged a connection between head injuries and its effects on the body, the ancient Egyptians had little understanding of the brain. Instead, the heart was considered the centre of intelligence and emotion. Physically felt beating at various rates during times of rest or excitement, its supreme importance was noticeable, especially when its cessation indicated death. The brain was likely considered to be mostly a substance to fill the space in the skull, and it was typically removed and not saved during mummification.

poured atop the entrails. Next would come the extraction of the other organs, minus the heart, with special attention also given to the liver, stomach and lungs, each in their own bowls to be separately desiccated. Mahu knew exactly where each organ lay, by location and feel, and expertly removed all, with not even the slightest nick marring the heart. Wads of linen were handed over and the slimy walls of the body cavity were wiped down with palm oil, the soiled cloth being stuffed into large white jars.

The next part had to be performed carefully as it could affect the appearance of the mummy's face. While an assistant held Amenhotep's head tilted back and rigid, Mahu grabbed a narrow chisel and carefully inserted it into the pharaoh's nose. A few expertly delivered taps with a wooden mallet were all that were necessary to make a breach that would give access to the interior of the cranium, where hooks and spatulas would aid in the brain's

## MUMMY BUSINESS

The word 'mummy' is derived from a Persian word for asphalt as the visual appearance of many mummies gave the impression that they had been coated in tar. The origins of mummification remain elusive. It's possible it was based on the observation of bodies that when interred in the desert (and then exhumed by wind or animals) had become naturally dried and somewhat resembled a once-living individual rather than a mere skeleton. At some point, artificial preservation became increasingly common and techniques developed to the point where it became a genuine industry. Mummification techniques varied through time and Egyptologists can sometimes determine the date of an individual by the method employed. In centuries past, ground-up mummies became a popular medicinal ingredient in Europe, and in the nineteenth century, it was possible for foreign tourists to return home from Egypt with a partial or complete mummy, and often its accompanying coffin, as a unique souvenir.

removal. Vigorously stirring some hooks and spatulas in order to break up the cerebral matter, a few bits and pieces came out in small chunks with the rest being liquified. The body was then flipped over, and the head held in such a way that whatever was left could drain out of the nostrils.

Palm oil was introduced and then drained out of the skull by flipping the body over, and finally, resin was poured in and the nostrils blocked with small rolls of cloth that would help retain the shape of the nose. Now free of internal organs, Amenhotep's body was washed again and his body cavity flushed with palm wine and aromatic oils. After introducing small bags of natron and a few bundles of linen to assist in retaining the hollowed body's form, the slit in the side was carefully sewn shut. His arms were crossed horizontally across his upper abdomen, and his body transferred to a wooden tray on which mounds of natron were poured, covering the deceased ruler from head to toe. There he would remain for weeks, before being elaborately wrapped and prepared for transport to Thebes for his interment in the royal cemetery about seventy days thereafter.

## THE OVERSEER OF WORKS

It didn't take long for the word to get out to a special and secluded village of workmen and their families. Called the 'Place of Truth', the unique community was set apart from the common population and provided a certain degree of secrecy to their primary task: constructing and decorating the tombs of the rulers. Situated in the Theban mountains, the royal cemetery was a relatively short hike from the village on trails that climbed along steep cliffs to a remote valley, ideally known only to a few. Initiated by Thutmose I about a hundred years previously, the valley known as the 'Great Place', or more impressively, the 'Good and Noble Necropolis of Millions of Years', seemed optimally positioned as a safe and easily guarded place where the royal bodies could rest unmolested for eternity. The location was further enhanced by a mountain resembling a pyramid rising above it all, providing the symbolic powers of those grand northern monuments built by the rulers of many generations past.

Life in the workmen's village could often be tedious, if not annoying, with stonecutters and artists living in close quarters, and their daily needs and payments supplied by the royal house. Food and even water were regularly delivered on donkeys and any disruption in supplies could be irritating. Amenhotep's grandiose tomb had been commissioned long ago and the work had been slow and steady. And with the talent available in the community, some of the more enterprising workers had been building their own tombs in the vicinity, dignified tombs that would surpass those usually accorded others of their station working elsewhere.

The rumours of Amenhotep's death had reached the village within days of the event, and the unannounced appearance of the Overseer of Works, Benia, accompanied by a couple of palace scribes early one morning confirmed

## THE VILLAGE OF THE TOMB WORKERS

The workmen's village supporting the royal cemetery is today known as Deir el-Medineh. Over the last hundred years, archaeologists have thoroughly excavated the extraordinarily intact site revealing great insights into the daily life of those who lived there, and Egyptian society as a whole. Apart from details of royal tomb construction, numerous written documents have survived relating to such things as personal relationships between individuals and the goods and services needed to sustain the village. Interestingly, a few of the best preserved and beautifully decorated tombs from ancient Egypt have been found within the village confines, having been built by the experts themselves, for themselves. The village was abandoned after the last royal tomb was constructed in the Valley of the Kings at the end of the New Kingdom.

it as fact. The ruler had indeed flown to heaven about a week previously and his tomb must be completed and made ready in about two months' time. The actual supervisor of work on the tomb, Kha, assured the Overseer that all would be ready. Most of the corridors and chambers were already largely finished, but there were still plenty of details to add, including preparing the walls and pillars of the burial chamber for decoration with essential texts and images.

Consulting with Benia, Amenhotep himself had approved the plans for his tomb not long after assuming the throne. It would be similar to that of his father, the third Thutmose, but slightly bigger and a little more elaborate. Positioned at the base of one of the valley's soaring walls, the tomb's entrance would begin with a set of steps leading down to straight sloping corridors interrupted by a deep rectangular shaft, which could both protect the workmen below in the rare event of a flash flood, and possibly thwart the efforts of future tomb robbers. After a couple of small storage chambers, the tomb's layout made a sharp left into a chamber with two pillars and stairs and a short corridor leading to the burial chamber.

THE EXCAVATED REMAINS OF DEIR EL-MEDINEH,
THE VILLAGE OF THE TOMB BUILDERS

Thutmose III's tomb had an oval burial chamber with two pillars and four side chambers, with its magnificent stone sarcophagus installed near its end. Amenhotep's plan retained the four side-rooms – in one of which he buried Prince Webensenu – but the chamber had straight-cut walls and six pillars, with the sarcophagus set in a niche in its floor. Benia insisted on seeing it all himself, and he and his entourage followed Kha along the trail leading up and over a ridge to the sacred valley. It had been a few years since the Overseer had made the trip, the last being during the installation of the sarcophagus, a difficult task from beginning to end. Although concentrating on his steps along the path, precariously close to fatal vertical drops, he couldn't help but admire the incredible view of green fields hugging the shores of the Nile and desert mountains off in the distance. The temple of Karnak could also be seen, with the gleaming obelisks erected by his predecessors clearly visible. Below were some of the memorial temples, including that of Amenhotep, something Benia would also be closely inspecting on the following day.

Passing several alert guards and reaching the edge of the Valley, Benia could see the dozens of animated workers at the entrance to the king's tomb, word no doubt having got out that his visit was imminent. The steep zigzagging trail into the Valley required caution but soon the construction site was reached. Taking a few moments to rest on a large flat rock, the Overseer asked to review the plans that had been drawn on a large sheet of papyrus paper being unrolled in front of him. 'So, every chamber is complete?  And the appropriate walls are as flat and smooth as possible, and ready to be plastered and painted?'

'Yes,' replied Kha.

'Very good,' replied the Overseer as he stood up. 'There isn't much time. I'd like to take a look.'

Two men with bowls containing oil-soaked wicks joined the visitors, providing the light needed for inspection as they traversed the tomb's initial descending corridors. The great pit had been filled temporarily with construction debris, which had enabled the incredibly heavy sarcophagus to be installed in the burial chamber. That material would be removed later after the funeral was complete. Benia was thus far impressed. Even though the tomb had been commissioned years ago, its immense size and quality explained its long construction time. Two well-organized gangs of workmen – one working on the left side of the tomb's corridors and chambers, and the other on the right – ensured that symmetry would be maintained throughout.

A left turn into a room with two pillars, some more steps and another sloping corridor led to the final chamber. The Overseer gravitated towards its latter part where the royal sarcophagus sat in a shallow sunken crypt approached by five descending steps. The great stone box was an incredible piece of work that few had ever seen, nor hopefully would ever see, especially after the tomb was shut, in all hope, for eternity. Carved from a single block of hard reddish-brown quartzite, it was a magnificent achievement in and of itself. Its head end was curved and its interior was sufficiently spacious to hold Amenhotep's coffin and mummy. A nearby matching stone lid would cover all. Benia knelt down and ran his hands along the smooth, polished sides of the sarcophagus, marvelling at its precisely incised decorations, each figure and hieroglyph lined with yellow paint. The protective goddesses Nephthys and Isis were represented on the head and foot ends as expected, and the sides bore texts and depictions of other deities who would protect the occupant. 'The Osiris, King Aakheperure, justified with the Great God,' he read to himself. Amenhotep was now becoming one with Osiris, the god of the dead, and his son, a living Horus, would take his place on the throne.

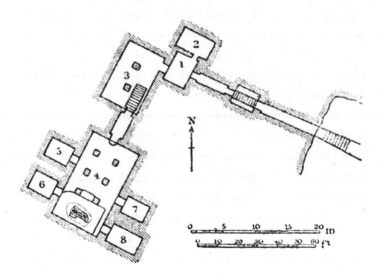

THE PLAN OF THE TOMB OF AMENHOTEP II IN THE 'GREAT PLACE', THE VALLEY OF THE KINGS

The Overseer got up and indicated that it was time to leave. On his way out, he stopped briefly at the one side-chamber already blocked shut. The burial of Prince Webensenu lay behind. Benia had watched him grow up. 'He was a fine young man, and might have been a great king,' he muttered under his breath, as he began his ascent to the light of the sun and fresh air outside.

Upon emerging from the depths, Benia addressed the assembled workmen. 'As I'm sure you know, the lower chambers are the most important, especially the walls and pillars in the burial chamber. You will plaster them first, and then a priest from the temple school will come with instructions and a scroll containing all that is to be painted on the walls. It is an extraordinary responsibility but I trust all of you will do it perfectly. And I will be returning to inspect everything before the funeral.' With that, Benia began his slog up the rocky slopes to the valley's rim to begin his journey back down to the workmen's village, with hopes of returning to his own home on the east bank of Thebes before dark.

Word that Amenhotep was dead brought seemingly everyone out in the streets of Baki's village. The reactions were mixed, with some crying if not quietly weeping, while others looked slightly forlorn. Ahmosi, the old amulet seller, paraded up and down the main village street shrieking to express what could very well have been sincere grief. Baki didn't care. He had just recently spent several obnoxious weeks assisting with the construction of Amenhotep's memorial temple, and what had the ruler done for him? He taxed his hard-won gains and ate better, lived better,

A GREAT REGAL SHIP PLIES THE WATERS OF THE NILE

and seemed to have a lot more fun. The ruler lived in opulent palaces in places like Memphis and Thebes, travelled the land in chariots and stately ships, and had legions of officials and servants to carry out his every command or whim. Still, Baki, as an Egyptian, recognized Amenhotep for what he was – a god in life and now a god in death – and pushed his less than pure thoughts out of his head.

Much of the talk around the town centred on two themes: cause of death and his replacement. With the dissemination of official information, it was clear that illness was the reason, rather than a bizarre accident or political intrigue. Regarding the latter, there had long been rumours that the current oldest son, Thutmose, was not the pharaoh's favourite choice, and an exception might be made in the usual manner of succession. Soon, though, the answer would be apparent to all.

The fishermen Nefer and Weni remained unperturbed as they sat at the Nile's edge. 'No matter who the ruler is,' commented the former unemotionally, 'I'll still be fishing every day, and little of that will change.'

# Fourth Month of the Season of Sowing and Growing

## THE CROWN PRINCE

Amenhotep's demise almost immediately stirred up controversy. Within moments of the ruler's body being removed to the embalming tent, the queen rushed forward to address the vizier. 'We must immediately announce the death of the ruler, and that all is well because Prince Thutmose is now pharaoh!'

'Tiaa, you know very well that the prince was not your husband's preferred choice as a successor, and he was on the verge of making a decision before he became ill. And I believe his selection was to be another capable son,' responded the vizier.

'Yes, but he did not declare his choice, and his eldest living son should be king. And did you not hear of Thutmose's dream? Horemakhet and the gods endorsed him!'

'Did the prince remove the sand encumbering the body of the Sphinx?'

'He is organizing it now!' insisted Tiaa.

Amenemopet was quickly interrupted as several of Egypt's highest officials gathered in the room. 'Proclaim to all that their beloved ruler, Aakheperure Amenhotep, has ascended to heaven, having died in battle with the demons of illness,' ordered the queen. 'Our new strong ruler is his son Thutmose, who will resume the maintenance of *maat* – truth, justice and order – immediately, and there is nothing to fear.'

At this announcement, the new king, now the fourth named Thutmose, emerged from a darkened corner and all bowed. Obviously nervous, he allowed his mother to speak on his behalf.

'Pairy, we would like you to remain vizier until Amenhotep is established in his tomb.' Speaking to Kenamun, the palace steward, she continued: 'You may remain and assist Thutmose in organizing his administration. And we will need to work hard on the details of the coronation. Taneny, as Overseer of the Army, you will respond should any of our enemies attempt to take advantage of the situation.'

Although Thutmose was now proclaimed the ruler, the tradition for the formal coronation was that it would take place on a very auspicious day, the next being the first of the new year, Wep-Renpet, over four months hence. During that occasion, Thutmose and his entourage would typically tour major towns and temples in the land to be crowned and embraced by his fellow gods. But for now,

A GRANITE SCULPTURE OF THUTMOSE IV AND HIS MOTHER, TIAA

there was some important business to attend to. 'Thutmose, listen to me!' whispered the queen to her son. 'Remove the sand from the Sphinx immediately! It must be done!'

## The Buried Sphinx is Uncovered

Just a week after Amenhotep's death, several large military ships moored at an ancient pier adjacent to the massive pyramids of Khufu and Khafre, unloading three hundred soldiers, most carrying large empty baskets and others shouldering wooden hoes. Aboard, too, was enough food and drink to sustain the men for at least the first few days, along with mats for sleeping and firewood to stave off the evening chill. When the order was given, the soldiers began the short hike to the giant protruding head of the Sphinx to immediately begin the arduous work of clearing sand.

Twenty of the men were placed side by side in front of the monument, with baskets at their feet and a hoe grasped and at the ready, and a long line of men stood behind each. With all organized, the process of freeing Khafre/Horemakhet from its sandy burial began. The hoes were used to pull sand into the baskets, which when filled were then quickly passed down the line to be emptied in an area sufficiently far away from the Sphinx so as not to make its reappearance when the excavation grew deeper. It was the job of a few of the workers to collect empty baskets and run them to the front, and those engaged in the strenuous wielding of the hoes were regularly substituted for others with fresher arms. A commander stood on a high spot with a few junior officers assisting him in the supervision of all. There would be no slacking, and the baskets were to be passed along full. With competent supervision and additional deliveries of fresh supplies, the task would be accomplished in just a few weeks.

## The Royal Funeral is Arranged

Back in the grand palace at Memphis, the work on the transition continued. It was important that the formal announcement of the new ruler must come quickly and be accompanied by his new royal titles, which were usually proclaimed at a coronation. For that, both the vizier, Amenemopet, and Amenemhat, the High Priest of Amun, convened with Thutmose for the essential task. With a senior royal scribe, Hututu, taking notes, the three began with the most important: the throne name. 'I have thought about this for a long time and prefer "Menkheperure", "Established Are the Manifestations of Re". I will be "Menkheperure Thutmose",' explained the former prince, 'very similar to my grandfather, "Menkheperre Thutmose".' The other two agreed that it wasn't a bad choice and then moved on to the other titles. After several hours of discussion, the final list was drawn up.

First was his Horus name: 'The Strong Bull, the Image of Appearances', and alternatively,'The Strong Bull, Beloved of Thebes'. The traditional 'Two Ladies' title came next, making reference to two female deities representing Upper and Lower Egypt, Nekhbet in the form of a vulture for the former, and Wadjet as a cobra for the latter. The title chosen was 'Stable of Kingship Like Atum', thus invoking the ancient god who created the other gods. Yet another title identified the ruler as the 'Golden Horus', and would likewise be powerful: 'the one great of strength who has repelled the Nine Bows', the Nine Bows being the traditional enemies of Egypt. The string of those titles would be in common use from then on, followed by both the throne and personal names of the new ruler.

With the selection of titles completed, orders were given to the chief scribe to record a message from Thutmose IV to be spread throughout Egypt, far and wide from north to south: 'This royal decree is brought to you to inform you that My Majesty – living, stable and healthy – has appeared as the King of Upper and Lower Egypt upon the Horus-throne of the Living, nothing of his like on earth. My titles are as follows. . .' After listing the Horus, Two Ladies and Golden Horus names, the letter continued. 'I will be known as The King of Upper and Lower Egypt, Menkheperure, The Son of Re, Thutmose. This letter is also to inform you that all is well and the palace is safe and sound.'

**THE ROYAL TITLES OF THUTMOSE IV**

Hututu hurried from the room with the letter to another part of the palace where a dozen scribes eagerly waited to produce their copies. All gathered around as the royal scribe slowly read the message several times. Accuracy was essential, and it was the most important document many of the scribes had ever written, and perhaps ever would. The numerous copies would be distributed to the governors of each of the forty-two provinces, and the highest officials in both Memphis and Thebes. This would hopefully assure all that, once again, Egypt was in excellent hands.

In terms of the royal funeral for Amenhotep, there was much to arrange. As with the great stone sarcophagus, there were several other important items that had already been produced and which lay in wait, because the ruler could potentially die from one thing or another at any time. There was a stately gold-gilded coffin, of course, to hold the wrapped mummy of the pharaoh, but also a special beautiful chest made from a single block of calcite. The box had four compartments, which would hold the pharaoh's four mummified and wrapped vital organs removed during embalming – the intestines, stomach, liver and lungs – and each compartment would be topped off with a lid in the form of the head of a protective deity representing each. The chest was in storage in a royal workshop in Thebes, and now would be shipped north to Memphis to receive its contents.

Overall, an inventory of hundreds of objects to be entombed with Amenhotep needed to be made, and their state of readiness known. If necessary, the royal workshops would be instructed to step up the pace of their work so all would be finished within a couple of months. There were to be gilded statuettes of various gods, figurines of servants eager to serve their master for eternity, chests with clothing and linen, furniture, large faience representations of royal and sacred symbols, and foodstuffs, plus wine and oils. And furthermore, but not least, there would be a large-scale wooden model of Amenhotep's beloved sailing barque, *Aakheperure Is the Establisher of the Two Lands*. So much work in so little time! With most of the items in production or stored in Thebes, Amenemopet knew he would be travelling southward very soon, and perhaps making the round trip between the cities several times.

The details of the grand funeral would also need to be arranged. One of the large royal barques would be adapted with a cabin for the coffin, and space for Tiaa and Thutmose, with other huge boats transporting other royal family members and high dignitaries. Notification of the boat's passage would be spread so that all those living along the banks of the Nile between Memphis and Thebes would have an opportunity to mourn. And then, the solemn transfer of Amenhotep and his grave goods to his tomb in the Great Place would require the utmost care.

## THE WEAVERS

In the village near Thebes, the two young widowed sisters were receiving increasing attention. With their long curly dark hair and gentle demeanours, they were found of interest by many single men, and perhaps even more so by their mothers. Tameret was sixteen when she was married and her sister Satmut fourteen, not unusual ages in a land where life was often short. Now, two years later, they lived in the modest house inherited from the older sister's deceased husband.

The two sisters were strangely quiet, uncharacteristic in the normal life of a village inhabited by commoners who were often noisy and animated. There were theories that part of their awkwardness was that being from far away in Lower Egypt, they spoke in a different way, pronouncing their words oddly at times, and sometimes they used terms that were not well known in the south. Some questioned why they hadn't returned to their homes in the north, but no one knew what awaited them there, or even if they could afford the journey. What was known was that they were still grieving and that they were both employed in the linen production facility near the flax fields.

Each morning, Tameret and Satmut would arise early and walk together towards their workplace clad in nothing more than a skirt wrapped around their waists; a common way of dressing for many of the women in the village, though sometimes accompanied by a shawl to wear over the shoulders during cool days or evenings. And while they were employed in a workshop that created some of the finest cloth used for the most sophisticated of garments, a few everyday skirts and a couple of simple tube-like dresses were all the two sisters owned, the latter to be worn only on special occasions.

The linen workshop was a very busy place, with all stages of cloth production in progress. Owned by the state, it received orders to turn out material that might be provided to all levels of society, from the coarse cloth that could be given to labourers as compensation or for cheap clothing, to the most exquisite, fine, white linen suitable for royalty and other elites of Egypt. The extensive neighbouring flax fields, also owned by the state, provided a ready source of raw materials.

Enclosed by large brick walls, dozens of people were actively employed in various tasks. In one corner of the compound were vast piles of yellowish flax stalks, which had been pulled out of the ground during the last harvest nearly eight months previously. Although the finest linen was produced from the younger, greener plants, the greater need was for more utilitarian cloth, and the abundance of fully mature flax and the thread derived therefrom kept the workshop busy all year round.

A number of men were involved in soaking stalks in a basin to soften things up before raking out the fibres with specialized combs used for that purpose. The thin fibres were then delivered in baskets to the spinners, who with their whorls could expertly transform raw materials into thread. From there, the thread went to the looms, where the cloth would be produced. Much of this work took place under a makeshift roof consisting of overlapping woven mats, which could protect the weavers from the distraction and heat of the bright sun as they focused on their tasks.

The workshop held several dozen looms, some of which were set up horizontally just above the ground. This

**WOMEN AT WORK IN A WEAVING WORKSHOP**

method had been in use for eons and was something to which most were accustomed. A more recent addition to the workshop were vertical looms, which had proven to be quicker and more efficient, with beams supporting upright threads to be interlaced.

Tameret and Satmut were assigned horizontal looms, where they quietly and skilfully warped and wefted all day long, just pausing for the workshop-provided midday meal of bread and beer. Being relatively new to the Theban area, they were assigned to producing the simplest and cheapest linen until proving their expertise to their supervisor, who might then choose to promote them to a higher grade of cloth.

After the sheets of linen were produced, another section of the compound consisted of a group of workers cutting the fabric into useful pieces, and producing simple garments requiring only basic sewing. Some of the best materials were sent elsewhere to be made into the finest of clothing. The two sisters never complained about work, and apart from the standard foodstuffs provided as pay, they were allowed a certain ration of cheaper cloth to be used in trading for other goods at the market. Some of the other workers were also widows, and they offered compassion along with helpful professional advice.

## TEXTILES

Although Egypt is known today for the high quality of its cotton, the plant was not utilized during most of ancient Egyptian times. Instead, flax was the dominant source of cloth along with the occasional use of goat hair and sheep's wool. One can identify a wide range of quality in the linen derived from flax, from the common and utilitarian, to the expensive and exquisite. An immense quantity of ancient linen survives in the form of mummy wrappings, and well-preserved garments have been discovered in relatively intact tombs such as that of Tutankhamun. Cotton first came to prominence during the early nineteenth century of our era, when large quantities began to be grown commercially and exported internationally to great acclaim.

## THE FISHERMAN AND THE HERDSMAN

At the river, Weni and Nefer were having a difficult day. First, they had a confrontation with a group of fowlers who interfered with their fishing by tossing their netted traps into the marshes to capture wild ducks, geese and other desirable birds. One of the traps caught on the prow of Nefer's skiff and when the fowlers pulled it in, his little boat was dragged rapidly into a papyrus thicket, tipping the skiff and knocking the fisherman into the water. Those on shore laughed, but Nefer wasn't amused; a basket of freshly caught fish had been lost in the process.

Reaching the shore, Nefer approached the men, who were removing trapped flapping ducks, some of which they were clubbing to death, while a few other birds were put into cages made from the woody parts of palm branches. The fisherman approached the first fowler in his way and shoved him to the ground. Grabbing a couple of the dead ducks, he walked off with the admonition: 'These might be worth a basket of fish. Watch what you are doing and stay away from us.'

The pushed man got up to fight but his friends held him back. 'You all smell like fish! And you will always smell like fish!' was the best he could muster.

Nefer handed one of the ducks to Weni with some good news: 'We're going to have a delicious meal this evening! My uncle only expects that we deliver fish to him and that's what we'll do. These birds are ours!'

Later that afternoon, the two had dropped their lines into the water when more trouble came out of the marshes. While sitting quietly, Weni was suddenly hit hard in the back by some sort of flying object. Looking into the water, he could see it barely afloat; it was a throwing stick, another tool used for fowling. Curved and smoothed, in the right hands it could strike one or more birds, which could then be retrieved in their stunned or deceased state. Looking over to identify the origin of the battery, Weni recognized User, a haughty, wealthy overseer, standing on his wider and more stable wooden version of their own papyrus skiffs. Punting with a pole, while his seated daughter assisted his balance by holding his leg, User would quietly approach a bird-infested thicket before launching his weapon. This time, however, he hadn't hit a bird.

The overseer manoeuvred over to the fisherman's skiff and could see his weapon floating away. 'Retrieve my stick at once,' he demanded, taking no interest in Weni who was clearly in pain. Nefer, who was nearby, was in no mood for the arrogance. Paddling over to the weapon, he fetched it and slowly approached User's vessel. 'You should be more careful where you fish!' admonished the overseer. As Nefer came close to handing over the throwing stick, he suddenly gave it a vigorous heave into a part of the marshy thicket that would make it nearly impossible to recover.

'You can retrieve it yourself and you can be careful where you fowl,' scolded Nefer. The fisherman then roughly splashed User and his daughter with his paddle, soaking them both, before tending to Weni whose back was clearly bruised. 'That roast duck tonight will make you feel better.'

A NOBLEMAN ENJOYS FOWLING IN A MARSH WITH
HIS FAMILY, A THROWING STICK IN HAND

Senna the herdsman had also had a bad day. That morning he had been kicked in the face by an angry cow as he knelt down to remove an acacia thorn from its rear leg. It certainly wasn't the first time, something made obvious any time Senna opened his mouth to speak or eat. The few teeth that remained in front were mere stumps. It was an accepted part of being a herdsman, an occupation with its own set of dangers, and virtually every part of Senna's body, at one time or another, had been kicked, butted or stepped upon. This time, the damage was relatively light, but still painful.

Senna, nonetheless, felt fortunate. He was responsible for a modest herd of about twenty short-horned cows, which unlike the long-horned varieties or some of the immense bulls were relatively docile and a few perhaps even endearing. There were tales of other herdsmen being gored or stomped to death by bigger creatures, but his, for the most part, rarely caused extreme incident. The cattle were owned by a wealthy estate owner who took special pride in his herd as they were a clear sign of his wealth and prestige, even among his peers.

Senna's job wasn't particularly difficult. Every morning he would emerge from his small shack on the estate and

## STRONG AS A BULL

The strength of bulls was highly admired and a reference to the ruler as 'the strong bull' was not unusual. In Memphis, an individual bull was selected and identified as the 'Apis', the living incarnation of the city's chief god, Ptah, and was treated with special deference as such. Upon its death, the Apis was mummified and buried in a huge stone sarcophagus in an underground labyrinth, and another bull was then selected that met the criteria to likewise be worshipped. In 1851, the subterranean cemetery of the Apis bulls was discovered at the site of Saqqara, the massive necropolis adjacent to the ancient city of Memphis. It's open to tourists who will likely find it to be an astonishing experience.

examine the herd before moving them out to graze. If there were any minor maladies or injuries, he would treat them and if there were pregnant cows, when the time came to give birth he would deliver their calves. Other than that, he mostly marched them to a place to forage, and then sat and made sure that all behaved, and that none ran away. The cows seemed to understand the routine and followed alongside Senna, who used a stout stick to guide them. Their owner had a section of his fields set aside as edible pasture but the herd could be moved elsewhere as needed.

Senna's kick in the face wasn't his only problem that day. While sitting at the edge of the estate owner's field, he had consumed a couple of jars of strong beer and drifted off to sleep, not noticing that one of his charges had been slowly separating itself as it continued to eat its way towards an adjoining property. Upon awakening, Senna felt something strangely amiss and counted the cows. One was missing. This was unacceptable and it raised the possibility that he could be harshly punished, or even worse, be accused of stealing. There was, however, another herd grazing nearby on an adjacent estate. Unfortunately, Senna had an uncomfortable relationship with its herdsman, Nebseny.

Senna called out to Nebseny who then counted his own cattle. 'That is a serious problem! There might be an extra cow here, but I don't remember if I brought thirty or thirty-one with me today. What does she look like?' Senna didn't appreciate the joke; all of Nebseny's cattle were white with black patches as were most of his own. 'Let's take a look,' he offered, and with little effort, he walked directly up to the errant cow, grabbed it by a short horn, and pulled it over to Senna. 'This must be yours. My cattle are more attractive and better fed.'

Nebseny laughed and took Senna over to several of his animals and pointed out that all had black circles painted around the base of their stubby horns. 'Mark your herd, Senna, and don't drink so much strong beer while you're working. Take your funny-looking skinny cow and return to the rest of your animals before they, too, run away to better pasture.'

Senna used his stick to prod the escapee back to his group before doing another count, relieved to find that all of the others were still there. The owner would never know what happened, nor would he need to know, as long as they were all available to show off and to slaughter on special occasions. 'Nebseny was right,' he concluded as he returned the cows to a penned area at the estate where they could be secured until the next day. He was right about both marking his cattle and about the beer. But the latter lesson could wait until the next day, as the beer might help kill the pain of his morning's injury.

As Senna sat in front of his shack, Mosi, the estate's beekeeper walked by the herdsman, who greeted him and offered him some beer. 'What happened to you, O Senna?' he enquired. Senna told his story and the beekeeper tried to be sympathetic. 'My face used to swell up like that when I was young and the bees would attack me. Now if I get stung I don't care and it doesn't bother me. And anyway, I think that the bees know me because they rarely sting me now.'

Mosi took a couple of sips of Senna's typically strong beer, and after both had consumed a few small jars, the herdsman felt comfortable sharing the story of his lost cow that day. 'How many bees do you have?' asked Senna, slurring his words. 'Do you count them? Do they wander around to other hives?'

After a few thoughtful moments, Mosi provided the only answer he could. 'There are too many of them, and they move too quickly to count, but there are plenty enough to do their job. Wait here, Senna, I'll be right back.'

The beekeeper disappeared into the darkness, and in a few minutes, he returned with a small container topped with a lid. 'Rub this on your face and on any cuts. Physicians use lots of our honey in their medicine. It should help you. And then much of our honey goes to the state bakeries and breweries. Bees and honey are special and I can tell you more about them!' And Mosi proceeded to do so, well into the night, even after Senna had long fallen asleep.

# First Month of the Season of Harvest

## THE RULER IS MUMMIFIED

Mahu approached the carefully guarded tray that held Amenhotep's remains buried deep in a mound of natron; the task of his mummification was finally coming to an end. With large pots at the ready, the white substance, much of it hardened into clumps from having absorbed bodily fluids, was carefully scooped off and deposited in the vessels. Gradually, the general shape of the former ruler was revealed, and with careful brushing, the details emerged. Although Mahu had embalmed thousands of deceased Egyptians over the last few decades, he felt both awed and nervous as he carefully examined the desiccated corpse. The nose hadn't collapsed; the finger and toe nails were intact; and the hair was in good shape, although in need of cleaning, as was the entire body.

Mahu's team jumped into action to gently wash away natron from skin surfaces before applying a thin coat of aromatic resin. The beautifully carved calcite chest had arrived a week before, and could now take receipt of the set of four embalmed organs, each of which had been removed from its drying in natron. Wrapped in linen, they were placed in the box with its four sections, with lids bearing the likeness of protective deities placed over each appropriate compartment.

The wrapping of Amenhotep himself would begin soon. Tiaa and the new king, Thutmose IV, could have asked to view the body before it was bound in the finest of linen, but they declined. A dried-out cadaver was rarely attractive and although it resembled the living pharaoh enough for its *ka* (soul) to recognize, it was no doubt better to remember the king at his healthy and animated best, and youthful and athletic as described and depicted on his statuary and monuments. Amenemhat, the High Priest of Amun, Amenemopet, the vizier, and the Chief Treasurer, Djehuty, all arrived for the final stages of the process, the latter bringing with him an entourage of heavily armed guards and other soldiers bearing several beautiful chests containing amulets and jewellery to adorn the body. The three officials were slightly taken aback at the sight of the dried, still, shell of their close friend, but agreed that his mummy was remarkable.

With a wealth of experience in such matters, Mahu donned a mask over his head in the form of the jackal-headed god of embalming, Anubis. There were traditional spells to be recited for each limb and body part as it was wrapped in strips of the finest linen, and Mahu knew each without hesitation. Apart from the vizier and the treasurer, there were few in the room who had ever seen the sheer quantity and quality of riches added to Amenhotep's body even before it was placed in its ornate coffin. Golden caps were placed over fingers and toes to keep those fragile bits intact, and a spectacular collar comprised of beads of coloured glass and polished gems was placed around his neck. As the binding continued, so did the spells, with the appropriate amulets wound into the mix. With the entire body wrapped, a solid gold mask was placed over the mummy's head, its shining visage projecting both authority and contentment.

## CANOPIC JARS

The containers holding a mummy's embalmed entrails are referred to by Egyptologists as 'canopic jars'. The name is derived from a Greek town in Egypt called Canopus where it was said that a special jar was worshipped as a god there. The jars typically come in groups of four, one each for the intestines, liver, stomach and lungs, and their lids are in the form of the human or animal head of the protective god for each organ. The inscriptions found on many of the jars typically include the name and titles of their owner and are especially useful when no other evidence exists from that individual.

Another group of well-guarded men entered the tent bearing an obviously heavy object concealed beneath a thick sheet. Set down gently, the covering was whisked away to reveal a startlingly beautiful coffin, its gold-gilded surface sparkling in the flickering light. Ineni, the master craftsman responsible for its manufacture, stood to the side, ready to accept praise or make any changes requested. Everyone was silent but for quiet gasps of amazement. Ineni had done a superb job and Amenemopet stepped over to congratulate him.

It now became a matter of placing the body into its coffin, with great hopes that with all the thick wrapping, the mummy would fit inside. The coffin's lid was carefully removed and with anxious anticipation, Amenhotep was

A SET OF CANOPIC JARS BELONGING TO A NEW KINGDOM
OVERSEER, C. 1427–1400 BC. THE ORIGINAL LINEN WRAPPING STILL
CLINGS TO THEIR INNER SURFACE

carefully set atop several linen strips, and then lifted above the exquisite box. Slowly and cautiously, the body was lowered into place. With little room to spare, the size was perfect, and Ineni breathed a sigh of relief.

Several stone vases of expensive unguents were brought forward and poured over Amenhotep before the coffin's gilded lid was set atop the box, and the tenons, pins and holes matched up to secure the two together. With the mummification complete and the body enclosed in its coffin, it was removed to the palace proper, along with the chest containing the dried entrails, and the large jars containing soiled linen and used natron. In just a few days they would begin a journey south to the Great Place for interment.

## A Book of the Dead is Commissioned

Amenemopet had had a busy couple of months. In charge of the final disposition of a dead god-king, he was responsible for ensuring that the tomb was completed and the funeral was properly organized. The entire matter caused the vizier to be introspective, contemplating his eventual and unpredictable death, which given his health, could come any day. The recent visit to his own tomb chapel was also concerning, and completing it was something else he needed to do. Upon reaching Thebes to pursue the royal arrangements, he called upon a local scribe who specialized in a certain kind of text. Nu was an expert in the writing of the Book of the Dead, a funerary scroll that would guide the deceased through the perils of the Netherworld and a successful judgement leading to a pleasant eternity.

Nu immediately recognized the vizier and listened to his concerns. 'So, you think you might die soon and you want a book,' summarized the scribe. 'It will be expensive, but it will serve its purpose. It has never failed!'

'How could he possibly know that!' thought Amenemopet sceptically, but no matter, he was only worried about himself.

'I will write the book, and it will be special for you, with your name written at the correct places, and realistic depictions of you in the Judgement Hall. It will take me a month or two but it will be the best you will find anywhere.'

The Book of the Dead, or more properly, the *Book of Coming Forth by Day*, was a costly luxury unaffordable by most, but the highest official in the land could certainly convince himself that it was worth whatever price he must pay. The book, inscribed on a long papyrus scroll, would be buried with him and be available for his guidance as needed. Arranged in dozens of chapters, there were spells to thwart tricksters, and advice on how to successfully pass the rigorous final judgement. Standing before the god of the dead, Osiris, seated on his throne and flanked by his two sisters, Isis and Nephthys, Amenemopet would be asked questions by forty-two assessor gods who would interrogate him about his behaviour while still living. Had he lied, robbed, uttered curses or caused anyone to go hungry? Had he fraternized with evil men, stirred up strife or inflicted pain? Had he stolen from the temple offerings or any other temple belongings? The book advises that he answer 'no' to each question.

A SCENE FROM THE BOOK OF THE DEAD DURING WHICH THE
DECEASED'S HEART IS WEIGHED AGAINST THE FEATHER OF
TRUTH. THE IBIS-HEADED GOD, THOTH, TAKES NOTE, WHILE THE
FEARSOME BEAST, AMMUT, EAGERLY AWAITS A FAILURE

The most vital part of the proceedings was the assessment of the deceased's worthiness by the weighing of his heart on a scale against the feather of *maat*, representing truth and goodness. The god Thoth stands by, pen in hand, taking notes while Ammut eagerly awaits. Ammut is a vicious composite creature with the head of crocodile, the body of a cheetah, and the hindquarters of a hippo. Should one's heart not be in balance with *maat*, it will be immediately gobbled up by the beast, thus dooming one to the ultimate punishment: non-existence for evermore. Success, though, means a delightful eternity.

'And what will this cost me?' asked the vizier.

'My usual fee: two healthy cows, five large jars of imported wine, a basket of fresh dates and a footstool made of the hide of a spotted cow.'

## A GUIDE TO THE AFTERLIFE

With its roots in the Old Kingdom 'Pyramid Texts' exclusive to rulers, and the later 'Coffin Texts' of the Middle Kingdom found inscribed on some of the coffins of the wealthy, the Book of the Dead became popular in the New Kingdom with those who could afford it. Written in scroll-form on papyrus paper, the book could include as many as 186 chapters. The books were typically individualized and some contain illustrations that specifically depict a scroll's owner. Many examples have survived through the ages to give us a glimpse of the ancient Egyptian journey towards the Afterlife.

'I think that can be arranged. Please begin immediately.'

Amenemopet's next task was to visit the tomb workmen's village, and in the company of Benia he set out in a chariot to meet Kha, the project supervisor, and inspect the status of Amenhotep's royal tomb. Meeting them there would be a representative from the temple library who would be bringing a very special scroll. The hike from the village to the Great Place was slow and taxing, with the vizier stopping numerous times to catch his breath during the climb to the cliff top, and his descent to the valley was assisted by two workmen bracing him by the arms. From there it was only a short distance to the opposite cliff, at the base of which could be seen a dark rectangular opening. Kha pointed out a precisely cut vertical shaft nearby. 'That's for you, O Amenemopet!' he explained. 'Just as Aakheperure Amenhotep promised! Your chapel will remain where it is in the nobles' cemetery, but you will eventually be buried here in the chamber below. Such a great privilege!' The vizier stared briefly into the deep hole, a shiver of pride lighting his face as he contemplated this honour. They continued on, passing between giant heaps of white limestone chippings flanking the entrance to the royal tomb, where his delegation was met by a trio of artists, along with a couple of the construction supervisors. The tomb itself was complete but for decoration, came the report.

The scroll from the temple library was rolled out on a large flat rock, to reveal the magical texts that would be written on the walls of the burial chamber. They belonged to the *Amduat: The Book of That Which Is in the Netherworld*, which mapped out the journey of Re, along with the deceased ruler, through the twelve hours of the night, to be reborn in the morning. Numerous gods and other-worldly entities are encountered; obstacles are met and overcome; and a fiendish enemy, Apophis, in the form of a snake, is defeated. The texts were accompanied by illustrations, and unlike the tomb of Amenhotep's father, Thutmose III, the chamber's six pillars would also be decorated with images of the ruler in the company of various gods and goddesses.

Amenemopet insisted on seeing that all was indeed in order, with the tomb cut well and the walls of the burial chamber nearly finished, with their coat of white plaster ready for painting. The vizier was impressed and expressed as much, and then added: 'You have only a few weeks to make sure all is ready, and you are to copy the texts and illustrations exactly as you find them on the papyrus!'

There was another matter of great logistical necessity for the upcoming royal funeral. 'We will need the way prepared for the transport of the coffin and grave goods. Benia, see that the old desert track is restored to the entrance of the valley. We certainly won't be carrying everything over the cliffs from the other side!' The track was a very long – but much less steep – trail between ravine walls that led up from the flat plain below into the Theban mountains. It had rarely been used since the funeral of Thutmose III and would require widening and repair.

'All will be done,' promised the Overseer of Works.

Enough of the path still existed at the valley's entrance, and donkeys awaited to take the visitors down to their next stop: Amenhotep's recently completed memorial temple. Reaching the bottom of the trail, the new monument could be seen from a distance, with its plastered white walls impressively shining bright. Built mostly of mud brick with stone accents, it featured two pylons, leading to a pillared courtyard. The vizier was impressed and Amenemhat assured him that rotations of priests were being organized to serve the temple with regular offerings in perpetuity.

There were just a few more places to visit including the storage rooms of royal funerary objects, and the workshops responsible for their creation. Much of the furniture fit for a king had been produced in the normal workshops or could be retrieved from the palaces, but many of the objects with special religious or funerary associations were

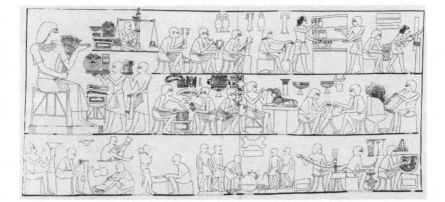

**A royal workshop produces funerary goods
including a gilded shrine**

stored in a well-guarded temple warehouse. Amenemopet was satisfied that all was sufficiently organized and the journey of the mummy to Thebes could begin.

In Memphis, a great gold-gilded wooden shrine had been constructed atop a sturdy wooden sledge, ready to house the royal coffin. A much smaller version held the chest containing the entrails. Captain Ipu was busy outfitting Amenhotep's favourite ship, the massive *Aakheperure Is the Establisher of the Two Lands*, which would be used to transport the mummy, along with a select few members of the royal family, and a small accompanying entourage, south to Thebes. On deck was a spacious cabin for the passengers, finely outfitted for comfort like a palace afloat. The great golden heads of Horus mounted on the upturned bow and stern were polished and any imperfections on the boat repaired.

With all ready, there was no need to delay. Amenhotep's coffin was installed in its gleaming shrine on the sledge as a procession was organized in the palace courtyard. High priests from the Memphis temples would lead the way with dozens of their underlings following behind, some carrying incense to perfume the air, and others carrying standards bearing the likeness of their gods. The coffin's sledge was next, hitched to a pair of huge matched bulls, and then the canopic shrine, which required only a single bovine. A large contingent of normally jovial priestesses appeared sombre and bereft, chanting a song of sorrow, and the best and most dramatic of professional mourners lined up to be followed by the royal family led by Thutmose and his mother in a chariot, along with some of the highest of officials. When the order was given, the gates of the palace were opened and the funerary parade began.

It wasn't far to the harbour, but the route was lined with thousands who reacted to the intense event, adding their cries to those of the mourners in the procession. The sight of the shrines was overwhelming and several in the crowd fainted at their appearance. The boat awaited, its crew standing sombrely aboard with Captain Ipu at the gangplank. As the din continued, the sledges were unhooked from the oxen, and several strong sailors pulled the great golden boxes on to the deck, where they were soundly fastened down.

The chanting and keening continued on the dock while the distinguished passengers boarded. With dozens of sailors manning their oars, Ipu gave the order to row the barque further into the Nile and then unfurl its massive sail for the journey upstream. The wind soon filled the sheet and the city walls of Memphis faded into the distance.

With luck, the voyage would take a week and a few days, depending on conditions, and including pausing briefly offshore at some of the largest towns or cult-places, such as Hermopolis, a town sacred to the god Thoth, and Abydos, the cult centre of Osiris. As they travelled, two women well adept at shrieking were stationed on platforms near the bow to alert the people of Egypt along the route, while a contingent of drummers aboard likewise made a racket, which also served to benefit the rhythm of the rowers. Captain Ipu preferred not to travel at night, as river obstacles including sandbanks required careful manoeuvring. Given the rare and precious cargo aboard, there could be neither accidents nor mistakes. The barque would anchor or dock each evening, and its eminent passengers would sleep in luxury, while the crew slept on the deck, ready to resume their efforts on the morrow.

## A Royal Funeral

Mutui had spent her entire life in the steadily growing village near Thebes. As a small child she had played in its streets and learned the skills of a homemaker from her mother. There she became acquainted with her husband, Baki, and was wed at age fifteen with the encouragement of her parents, who had likewise met in the same village. Mutui and Baki were both attending one of the local festivals when they found themselves attracted to each other. The young woman was impressed by the somewhat older farmer and his sturdy physique. Baki, in turn, found Mutui beautiful and was charmed by her flirtatious and witty remarks.

After six years of marriage, there had been, thus far, four births, but only two of the babies survived, one being now three years old and the other four. Baki hoped for more boys who would eventually help in the fields as he grew older. He and Mutui were confident that there would be more babies to come.

Life was fairly routine and busy for Mutui, but not necessarily arduous. She arose before dawn each day to make sure the family would have its bread and a first meal, and then the rest of the day would be filled with caring for the children, sewing as needed, more meal preparation, and tending to her small garden. The garden consisted of a rectangular raised bed enclosed by low mud-brick walls. Located behind the house, onions, radishes and lettuce grew nicely there and Baki regularly provided jars of water for their maintenance. Between the vegetables and the substantial granary well-supplied from the harvest, her family was essentially self-sufficient, with both surplus grain and vegetables being available to trade for other items.

On one particular day, Mutui was down by the river washing her family's clothing, pounding out mud and other stains on some smooth rocks in the company of a dozen other women. It was a favourite time of the day, with an exchange of news and gossip that kept things interesting. The small children played nearby and with all of the women watching, there were regular admonishments to stay away from the water; the currents and the creatures of the Nile were not to be taken lightly.

While engaged in lively conversation that day, an odd rhythmic noise was heard in the distance, accompanied by what seemed to be high-pitched screams. Its intensity increased with every moment, and within minutes, small regal boats with sails aloft and rowers in motion appeared, with drummers alerting all to pay attention. In their wake the massive royal funerary boat appeared, its shrines shining on deck. There were few in the village who didn't rush to the riverside to observe the spectacle as the great ship passed on its way to its final berth at the Theban royal dock, and like a giant sonic wave coursing its way along the Nile's banks, the wailing amplified as the villagers realized what they were witnessing.

Mutui was stunned and overwhelmed with unanticipated emotions. She was soon joined by Baki who had occasionally made snide comments about the former ruler, but likewise felt awed by the pageant. The farmer's entire life thus far had been experienced under the rule of the Lord of Upper and Lower Egypt, Aakheperure Amenhotep, for better or for worse, and he surprised himself when he shed a brief tear. Many standing on the shore joined the cacophony, some of the women even pulling at their hair in anguish and throwing dust in the air. The glorious barque docked in front of the royal palace, and the deceased pharaoh would make his final physical journey on the very next day.

Re had barely risen on the horizon when Amenemopet stood in the courtyard of the great Theban temple of Amun to organize a procession nearly identical in composition to that which had recently occurred in Memphis, but on a much larger scale. The logistics, too, were significantly more complex. A suitable spot on the west bank had been prepared to receive the royal ship, and the members of the entourage themselves would need to regroup on that side of the river. All of the royal funerary equipment was arranged for the big day and the tomb itself readied to receive its occupant.

With the sledges removed from the barque and hitched to strong bulls, and the hundreds of the invited elite in place, the solemn yet noisy procession began, led by the High Priest of Amun, Amenemhat, along a smooth and broad path lined with spear-bearing soldiers. As before, Thutmose rode in his chariot, Tiaa at his side. The first stop was Amenhotep's just-completed memorial temple where the sledges were pulled into the courtyard. The newly appointed priests of the temple stood in a row, chanting recently composed hymns of honour, and presenting the expected offerings.

The provisions to be interred in the tomb had been gathered within the temple's interior, and after this brief stop, most of those who had participated to that point were dismissed; the journey to the sacred valley and the royal burial were only for the most privileged, as selected by Thutmose and his mother, with the advice of Amenemopet. These select few were to be accompanied by a contingent of specially chosen priests and facilitators, and the most trusted of workers chosen to bear the items to be installed in the tomb.

Again, the vizier organized the line-up, with Thutmose in the lead followed by royal family members, the high priest and the select few. The shrine-sledges came next followed by a long line of bearers, many from the village of tomb workers, who were to carry the hundreds of items to accompany Amenhotep in his grave. Intermixed were a select group of shrieking professional mourners to ensure that grief was majestically expressed. Following first a course along the base of the Theban hillsides, the track made a sharp uphill left turn before the final gentle ascent to the sacred valley.

The journey only took about an hour, and for most, it was their first visit to the valley. The sun shone brilliantly overhead while the pyramid-shaped mountain never failed to impress. Amenemopet stepped forward to greet Benia, who assured him all was ready and then stepped quickly away as Thutmose exited his chariot to lead the way to his father's tomb. The new ruler instructed the vizier that a single and brief nose-touching-the-ground obeisance was all that was to be required by the workmen on this special occasion, as there was plenty of work to be done without the expected excessive grovelling.

The oxen pulling the sledges were brought forward to the broad approach at the mouth of the tomb, and then unhitched and taken aside to await their fate. The bearers of the funerary goods were told to sit and keep quiet while the larger shrine was opened, and the gilded royal coffin removed and stood on end. From there, Amenemhat took over, directing the ceremonies, which in many ways resembled those performed for the elite, but adapted for the burial of a deceased god-king. The lector priest read from his script, and a small choir of priests and priestesses chanted and sang. The Opening of the Mouth ritual was performed and then the time arrived to transport Amenhotep to his stone sarcophagus waiting in the tomb's underground chamber.

The coffin was then lifted by several of the strongest workers, who followed Thutmose, Amenemopet and Amenemhat into the depths. The way was dimly lit but manageable if taken slowly, and after passing over the rubble-filled shaft and through the small two-pillared room, they reached the burial chamber awaiting its occupant. The vizier was impressed; the artists had painted the walls and pillars exactly as planned, the texts and illustrations of the *Amduat* looking exactly as if a giant papyrus scroll had been unrolled and affixed to the room's walls.

Amenhotep's coffin was gently lowered into the great stone sarcophagus, its face staring at the ceiling, which had been painted to resemble the sky with brilliant golden stars against a dark blue background. Amenemhat requested a couple of jars of funerary unguents as a final anointment of the dead ruler. Reciting prayers under his breath while pouring out the viscous liquids, Amenemhat was joined by two priests who stepped forward to place floral wreaths atop the coffin. With that, Thutmose and the others turned to make the trip back to the surface.

Outside, the bulls who towed the sledges had already been slaughtered and butchered and a feast was in the making. While the bulls were roasting, chairs were set up and mats laid out with the finest food Egypt had to

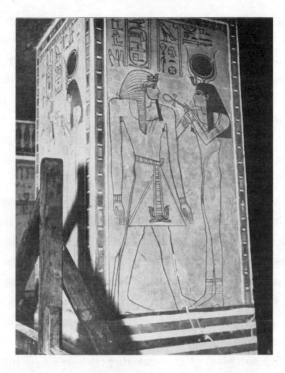

AMENHOTEP STANDS BEFORE HATHOR AS DEPICTED ON ONE
OF THE DECORATED PILLARS IN THE ROYAL TOMB

offer. Although still mourning, the guests, bedecked with
splendid garlands around their necks, enjoyed what was
now becoming somewhat festive. In the background, the
workers were busy bringing the tomb's provisions to be
installed in the rooms extending from the burial chamber.
One room would contain food and drink, while another
was filled with figures of gods and other items of religious
significance, and another would hold a variety of other
items suitable for a pharaoh's Afterlife including dozens

of exquisitely produced servant statues anxious to serve. The fourth chamber had already been utilized a few years previously for the burial of Webensenu. The shrine from the sledge was dismantled and carried inside, where it would be installed around the great stone box before the tomb was closed. The smaller sledge with the shrine containing the canopic chest was towed down below, to take its place close by the sarcophagus.

With the funeral guests well sated, Thutmose insisted on one last look at his father's coffin. With Tiaa on his arm, the two descended to the august chamber where the silence was nearly overwhelming. Holding back tears, the queen gazed in the inlaid eyes of the golden coffin, now glistening from the unguents. Removing her garland, she added it to the others before turning away. 'We'll see him again, won't we, my son? Someday?' she asked. Thutmose didn't answer. Amenhotep was dead and gone, at least from the earthly realm, and there were more pressing things for a living ruler to do.

Chariots to carry the funerary participants awaited at the entrance of the valley to deliver the sad and pampered back to Thebes. Meanwhile, the incredibly heavy stone lid of the sarcophagus was levered into place; the gilded shrine from the sledge was erected to surround it; and afterwards a stone wall was quickly built to block the lower portions of the tomb. A couple of workmen stepped forward with dishes of white plaster and soon the wall was completely smoothed over, looking almost as if the tomb itself ended at that very spot. Outside, the many bearers and other workers devoured the leftovers from the banquet. It would be a tiresome walk back to their villages, but at least they did so with satisfied stomachs and memories of an event witnessed by few.

In the next few days, the shaft would be emptied of its loose debris and the entrance to the tomb blocked and plastered. Benia and Kha, in the presence of Amenemopet, would stamp the damp plaster with the seal of the royal cemetery and the cartouches of Aakheperure Amenhotep, in a final act that they hoped would protect the great warrior pharaoh for eternity.

# Second Month of the Season of Harvest

## THE NEW RULER

Thutmose sat on a beautiful ebony chair in the bedroom of the Memphis palace. It seemed to be one of the few remaining objects bearing his father's name incised in gold leaf or inlaid with precious materials. Although much was buried in Amenhotep's tomb, enough still remained and the new ruler concluded that it was time to make Egypt truly his own. Early in the month, he called Amenemopet forward to inform the vizier that in the aftermath of the royal funeral, his services were no longer needed. New high officials would need to be appointed as would many others to form Thutmose's administration.

Amenemopet had heard rumours of this in advance so it was no surprise. It was actually a relief. The great vizier had watched Thutmose grow up from birth and had little interest in advising someone he still considered a child, albeit that of his dearly departed friend. 'Do let me know if you need any advice,' offered Amenemopet as he exited the room. With deteriorating health, he likely wouldn't live too much longer, but at least he could retire in luxury at his villa, free from the formidable responsibilities of his office, and content that he had performed his duties well. In fact, it would take more than one to replace him.

Ruling Egypt was a complicated affair, and transitioning from a life of sporting adventures to maintaining order in the universe was an intimidating prospect. With Amenemopet dismissed, Thutmose appointed two new viziers, Ptahhotep and Hepu, one each for Upper and Lower Egypt. And as was the case during his father's reign, there would also be a 'Viceroy of Kush' who would look over Egypt's affairs with its adversarial southern neighbours in Nubia. Some of the old officials would be kept in place, but many would be replaced and others added; a god-king was free to choose his administrators.

Thutmose called Ptahhotep into his room. 'This is my palace now. I would like new furniture, new tapestries, new ritual objects, and even new chariots, all bearing my royal cartouches. And I'd like my father's boat renamed. It will now be called *Menkheperure Is the Establisher of the Two Lands*. Also, I want the finest stonemason in Egypt to report to me at once.'

'It will be done,' promised the fresh vizier as he was dismissed.

A few days later, Anen the stonemason arrived, to be greeted by Ptahhotep. 'His majesty has a very important task for you to accomplish. It will be a large stone stele [tablet]. It will be large enough to stand prominently between the recently cleared paws of the Great Sphinx at Giza. You will carve the text accurately as presented to you and it will be executed in the finest manner possible.'

Anen looked at several sheets of papyrus paper that had been pasted together to form a short scroll. The many lines of script were complex but certainly within his abilities.

The text of the stele had been carefully discussed by a small committee composed of Thutmose, his mother, the high priest Amenemhat and the two new viziers. It was Tiaa's idea. Carved literally in stone, and erected in front of one of Egypt's most imposing monuments, it was hoped that it would settle any questions about the legitimacy of Thutmose's right to the throne. His name and several of his titles would be prominent and the story to be told would be indisputable.

Amenemhat conducted the meeting with a summary of the text to be carved on the great stele. Addressing Thutmose, he said, 'We'll begin with a statement by Horemakhet that you have indeed been granted kingship and awarded might by the gods. We'll note that you were a beloved young man, and like your father, a true athlete. At various places you will be called by your many majestic titles, "gleaming of diadems", "mighty bull" and "stable in kingship like the god Atum", accompanied by mutual praise between the gods and yourself. But the most important part will be the story of your divine dream that took place at that very sacred spot in the presence of your great ancestors. Here's a short version for now:

'It happened one day that the king's son, Thutmose, was travelling on the Giza plateau around noontime. He sat down in the shadow of the Sphinx and fell asleep when the sun was at its highest. The great god Horemakhet spoke to the sleeping prince as a father speaks to his son. "Look at me, my son, Thutmose! I am your father, who has given you kingship upon earth and put you in charge of all living. You will wear the Red and White crowns of Upper and Lower Egypt. All of this land is yours, and is in your hands to maintain. All the tribute of foreign lands is yours and you shall live and reign for many years."

## THE DREAM STELE

The impressive granite stele of Thutmose IV still survives between the paws of the Great Sphinx of Khafre at Giza and has been given the name the 'Dream Stele'. It stands 3.6 metres (12 feet) tall, and made of heavy granite, it weighs 15 tons. Most of its informative text is legible but part of its lower section has deteriorated. Despite ancient efforts to remove the sand from around its body, the Great Sphinx probably spent much of its existence encumbered up to its neck. The last major clearance was conducted by archaeologists beginning in 1926, and since then the Sphinx has been well studied, conserved, and remains a popular tourist attraction.

'And then the part about the repairs,' continued Amenemhat. 'Horemakhet speaks and calls attention to the woeful state of his great monument buried in sand: "I have waited for you to come and do what needs to be done as you are my son and protector, and I am your guide."'

'How long will this project take?' enquired the ruler.

'Anen, the stonecutter, tells me it will take five months,' explained the vizier. 'There was a choice of limestone, sandstone or granite. I selected granite. Even though it will take longer, it should last for eternity.

'Begin the project immediately,' ordered Thutmose, 'and it will be completed and installed between the paws of the Sphinx exactly five months from today.'

## THE FISHERMAN COMPOSES A LOVE POEM

It was just another beautiful day on the riverbank as the fishermen prepared for work. Weni and Nefer would be taking their skiffs out to work with a net together, and perhaps even harpoon anything especially large that might reveal itself with a loud splash. When it came time to enter the water, though, Weni was untypically slow, and when he tossed the net between the two little boats, he missed several times. 'Are you not feeling well?' asked Nefer. 'You seem very distracted.'

'Oh, Nefer!' answered Weni. 'I am ill with love. I can't think of anything other than Tameret the weaver. I can't even think of fish! She is so beautiful. She shall be my wife!'

THE GREAT SPHINX AT GIZA AS SEEN IN MODERN TIMES
WITH THE 'DREAM STELE' VISIBLE BETWEEN ITS PAWS

The two got to work, although there was a distinct lack of the necessary coordination, and after rounding up a couple of dozen small perch, Nefer lost his patience and decided to fish on the shore alone with a line.

'I have an idea, Nefer!' proclaimed Weni. 'I will write her a lovely poem that will show her how I feel. She will be so impressed. I have already started it in my head:

*Tameret. I love you more than fish.*
*I admire you more than my friend, Nefer.*
*Your curly hair reminds me of our nets,*
*and your body is finer than that of the finest talapia.*
*My love for you would fill five large baskets.*

'I will leave the poem on the doorstep of her house for her to find and then seek me.'

'I see some problems here,' offered Nefer. 'I don't think she'll be impressed by all of the fishing references, but more importantly, you don't know how to read or write, and she probably doesn't either.'

After a few minutes of contemplation, Weni came up with an idea. 'Oh, Nefer! I have an idea. I will consult a scribe. Senna the herdsman knows some. Remember at the wedding of his son? Two of them came. I will bring him a couple of these perch today and ask him for a favour!'

At the end of the work day, Weni ran up to the edge of the field, a couple of fish dangling from a cord slung over his back. Senna was just returning from the field with his herd when the fisherman approached. After explaining the situation, Senna gave it some thought. 'It will take more than these two fish. Give me some more later and I'll see what I can do.' Weni thanked the herdsman and returned home, elated with hope.

Just two days later word reached the fishermen that a stranger was waiting at the edge of town, requesting the presence of Weni. It was Dagi, the junior scribe who had accompanied Minnakht to the wedding celebration. 'I understand that you need some help writing a love poem.'

'Yes, yes, O scribe. A poem to proclaim my love to the most beautiful girl in Egypt. A poem that she will read and then will want to marry me!'

'Can she read?' came the anticipated question.

'I don't know,' responded Weni, 'but maybe her sister can.' Dagi was sceptical but as he was sent by his boss, Minnakht, he decided that the fewer questions the better.

As the two sat down on the trunk of a fallen date palm near the road, Weni began to recite his poem. 'Tameret. I love you more than fish. I admire you more than my friend, Nefer. . .'

Dagi called a quick stop to the recitation. 'That is very nice, Weni, but I think we can do even better than that. Let's try this:

*Lovely Tameret:*
*When I see you, my heart is joyful without beer,*
*When I hear birds singing beautifully in the marshes,*
*I wonder if it is your voice.*
*When I am at the river, my eyes long to see you bathe in*
    *a dress of the finest linen,*

*while I await on shore with a towel to dry you.*
*When you walk by, the flowers bend slightly in hopes*
  *that you will pluck them,*
*and place them in your soft and scented hair.*
*In the market, my heart detects your sweet perfume*
  *before you appear.*
*Fairest one, my life's greatest desire is that you will share*
  *my love,*
*And we will live long and happy together.*
*I, Weni, am a simple fisherman but I will treat you like*
  *the queen you are.*

'How is that, Weni?' asked the scribe.

'That is excellent! I will leave it in front of the door of her home this afternoon!'

'Here, Dagi, please take this basket of fish as it is all I have to offer. I'll ask Senna to deliver it to your home. He has a donkey.'

'Good! He has a donkey, you have a poem, and I have fish. We are all content. Good luck with love, Weni,' replied the scribe as he packed up his writing kit and quickly strolled away.

That afternoon, Weni took the sheet of papyrus paper, rolled it up, and carefully tied a bit of string around it before depositing it against the door of the widows' house. The sisters would surely find it when they returned from the weaving workshop later in the day, and they did. The little scroll was nearly stepped upon before Tameret noticed it at her feet. Carefully unrolling it, the two sisters could only speculate about its source and content. Could it be a letter from their village in Lower Egypt? Were they in trouble? It made them both nervous and it wasn't until the next day that a kindly overseer at the workshop agreed to read the message. He smiled as he recited the flattering lines: 'Lovely Tameret. . .'

## The Valley Festival

It was the first full moon of the tenth month, and it was time for another annual event welcomed by many, but best appreciated by the elites of the Two Lands. It was the Valley Festival, during which the grand deities of Thebes would cross the Nile to its west bank and pay visits to the memorial temples of several of Egypt's rulers. Like the Opet Festival, the images of Amun, Mut and Khonsu would be carried from their respective temples in shrine-bearing barques, borne on the shoulders of sturdy priests, accompanied by an exuberant entourage.

At Karnak, the high priest, Amenemhat, was once again providing instructions to the assembled priests who had been selected for their uniform height and strength. The barque of Amun should not be dropped, of course, nor should the other two. And like Opet, the festival would have its own special logistical requirements. The barques would be transported to the river and put aboard ships made ready for them. Upon reaching the other side, they would travel up canals to bring them closer to the temples. Then, they would be borne on human shoulders again to be carried to their destinations on land.

The festival would last but a couple of days and the itinerary was intense. Apart from the initial rituals to take place at Karnak before departure, there would be several stops on the west bank with brief visits to the memorial temples of earlier rulers including those of Thutmose III and the recently deceased Amenhotep II. The priests associated with each temple had spent weeks preparing, and for them it was perhaps the most important occasion of the year.

For those whose relatives had been able to afford to be buried in the elite cemetery, the tomb chapels of the deceased would be visited, offerings and flowers presented, and a feast celebrated. As the ultimate high priest of all of Egypt's temples, the new king, Thutmose, would be actively involved and would conduct at least gratuitous rituals at the various sites to be visited.

With everyone in place, the festival began in the morning with the well-guarded Thutmose leading the way from the great Amun temple in his gilded chariot for the short trip to the docks. The barques came next accompanied by the usual assemblage of chanters, musicians and dancers. Maatka, a priestess of Hathor, would be among them. The noise continued as all were loaded on the boats for the short trip across the river, to be greeted by a joyous welcoming throng.

Maatka had served her goddess for over a dozen years, mostly attending festivals where she sang and danced in her honour. The subject of her devotion, Hathor, the daughter of Re, had many personalities and could sometimes have the mothering nature of a cow, as she was often depicted, and then transform into Sekhmet, one of the fiercest goddesses known in Egypt. Depicted in the form of a lioness, Sekhmet's anger could be swift and brutal. Her viciousness was displayed in a story with which Maatka was well familiar.

After observing how disappointed her father was with the behaviour of humans, Hathor in the form of Sekhmet went on a killing spree, destroying any humans she might encounter. Re was appalled and concocted a trick to end the rampage. Great pools of red beer resembling blood were created to which Sekhmet was attracted, and as she drank, she became drunk and fell asleep, and awoke in a better mood. It was no wonder that she was also the goddess associated with drunkenness! As was expected, Maatka participated in a particular event dedicated to that very thing, the annual Tekh Festival, which honoured Hathor's role as such. Massive quantities of beer and wine were consumed, and other usually prohibited behaviour was tolerated in a kind of communion with the goddess. Although Maatka once looked forward to its annual excesses, it was becoming less interesting as recovery from the occasion with all of its side effects became less tolerable.

Despite her declining interest in Hathor's wilder side, Maatka still very much enjoyed the dancing during the festivals, and considered her own rattling of a hand-held metal Hathor-headed sistrum to be exceptional, as well as her subtle shaking of a special bead necklace, which was said to be pleasing to the goddess. Given her years in service, Maatka no longer felt comfortable engaging in the spirited somersaults, back-flips and other tumbling manoeuvres expected while marching alongside the transport of divine barques, or during other festive occasions. Instead, she served as a mentor to dozens of young women who themselves dreamed of being one of those attractive and fit priestesses of Hathor. Not all had the prerequisite physical flexibility, musical sense of rhythm, an engaging personality or the ability to consume large quantities of alcohol, but those who did could expect a degree of respect and subsistence courtesy of Hathor's temple. Maatka did her best to contribute her skills to the Valley Festival's great processions, stopping to eat and drink heavily at several locations along the way, and encouraging her protégés to follow suit.

The now-retired vizier, Amenemopet, had participated in the Valley Festival many times over the years, but this one would be special. Not only did he visit the temple dedicated to his lifelong friend, Amenhotep, but he also honoured his deceased brother, Sennefer, in the courtyard of his impressive tomb chapel. There were plenty of good friends and relatives present, and the outdoor banquet was superb. A party nearby, at the tomb of the vizier Rekhmire, was likewise extravagant, crowded and joyful.

Much to his continuing embarrassment, however, was the unfinished state of his own tomb. Little progress had been made since his last recent visit, but as he was no longer working, there was now an opportunity to focus on the task in the months, and possibly years, ahead. None of the guests seemed to notice, and for Amenemopet, the feast was the most satisfying in memory.

## Thutmose Commissions his own Royal Tomb

A week after the Valley Festival, the Overseer of Works, Benia, was called to the palace. Thutmose awaited with Ptahhotep and the ruler described a special project: his burial place in the royal cemetery was to be initiated immediately. Kha, who would supervise the work, would join the three on the very next day as they discussed its location in the sacred valley, and the general plan of the tomb. With the track up to the Great Place still in good shape after Amenhotep's recent funeral, the journey in chariots was relatively easy, and the valley stood silent and empty of workmen. Kha and an accompanying scribe sat alone, waiting for the pharaoh and his small group to appear.

As Thutmose eventually approached, Kha knelt down with his nose to the ground as was expected. With a wink at Ptahhotep, the new ruler kept Kha on his knees for a moment or two longer than normal to demonstrate his authority before ordering the senior tomb builder to his feet. 'I am here to begin the construction of my place of eternity,' he explained unnecessarily.

'As you command, it shall be done,' answered Kha, 'in that we can carve out a marvellous tomb in the superb limestone of this very special valley, and we can facilitate the construction of a magnificent sarcophagus as the eternal resting place of your majesty's divine body. And I know a perfect place for the entrance to your tomb!'

Kha led Thutmose and his entourage to an area along one of the valley's high vertical walls, not far from the tomb of Amenhotep II. Thutmose was not impressed. 'My father was a great man in life, and I will be constantly compared to him in life and death. I prefer that my tomb be situated in another part of the royal cemetery!' he insisted. Kha was prepared for as much and guided the group to a cliff on the opposite side of the valley, conveniently not too far from where the trail from the workmen's village dropped down. It was a quiet and serene location, with only the occasional swoosh of a bird overhead to interrupt the natural silence.

## THE TOMB OF THUTMOSE IV

Known today as KV 43 ('Kings Valley tomb number 43'), the tomb of Thutmose IV is very similar to that of his father, Amenhotep II (KV 35), but larger in several dimensions. Curiously, only a few walls were decorated, none being in the burial chamber. The quartzite sarcophagus is indeed massive, being over 3 metres (10 feet) in length, more than 1.5 metres (5 feet) in width, and over 1.8 metres (6 feet) in height. An informal inscription on one of the tomb's walls indicates that its burial had been robbed only about seventy years after its initial closure, and then 'restored' on orders of the then-ruling pharaoh. When discovered by Howard Carter in 1903, he found that the tomb had been ransacked a second time by ancient robbers but much of interest still survived.

'This place is very pleasing to me. Make my tomb here,' ordered the pharaoh. 'Make it similar to that of my father, but bigger. I especially liked his burial chamber with its six pillars, and four side-chambers. What I did not like was the size of his sarcophagus; it seemed so small for such a great and long-lived ruler. I would like one made of the same kind of stone, quartzite, but much larger; large enough to contain the remains of one even greater.'

Kha was a bit taken aback at the presumptuousness of someone barely declared king but it was not his place to question such things. His job was to recommend, and to deliver to the specifications of royal commands. 'It will be done as you have requested,' replied the overseer.

'Begin the work immediately,' commanded Thutmose as he turned to walk away. 'Who knows when I might die?'

As the visiting party moved on, Kha was a bit shaken. He had never been treated in such a dismissive way, and worse yet, he had some unwelcome news for the residents of the royal tomb workers' village. Their short rest after the burial of Amenhotep was over, and it was now time to begin the process anew. The rough carving-out of the tomb's entrance would begin the very next day. The plan to follow would be that of their last project, although slightly enlarged, and its features adjusted as the physical situation might require.

The great stone sarcophagus was another matter altogether. It would need to be quarried as a single block from a source of the best stone, which was situated a few days' sail south. Between the shaping, hollowing and finishing, the work would take many, many months, and the end result would weigh many tons. The accompanying lid would likewise be a major, and heavy, project of substantial effort. Returning to his village, Kha announced the new project and quickly dismissed any complaints, reminding the workers that their job was to build royal tombs and such, for which they were supported by the palace. There were certainly other jobs far worse, and far less prestigious, and those who grumbled too much could be replaced.

# Third Month of the Season of Harvest

## THE COMMANDER AND THE CAPTIVES

One day, after being in his job for about a month, Hepu, the new vizier for Lower Egypt, made his way to the palace in Memphis. Although he had served in a number of administrative capacities for years, being in charge of half of the Two Lands was intimidating, as the position presented regular challenges. Today would certainly be interesting. Hundreds of captives had arrived from Canaan with their fates to be determined. It was a responsibility that weighed heavily on the vizier as the majority would be assigned to exceptionally miserable jobs, often alongside convicted criminals. 'They're not Egyptians,' he justified to himself insincerely, 'and some of them actively rebelled and are lucky to be alive.'

Reaching the great walls of the palace and gaining

admission to its inner rooms, Hepu approached Thutmose who stood looking out of a window.

'Your majesty, I have some reports for you and there are big decisions to make today.'

It was becoming clear to the new ruler that his days of a free-spirited, relatively easy life were mostly over.

'All is in order, but a ship loaded with loathsome Canaanites arrived yesterday, and they await your judgement.'

'Let me see them!' commanded Thutmose.

Hepu left the room for a few moments to whisper to an assistant, and then returned. 'Your majesty, look into the courtyard.' Down below, three rows, each consisting of 120 bearded men tied to one another, were marched in, their elbows tied behind their backs, and their heads bent forward. Occasional blows from a rod-wielding soldier kept things moving until all were in view.

'Down on your faces!' ordered a commander, and all dropped to their knees on the brick pavement, with their noses painfully bearing too much weight without arms for support. 'Keep your eyes shut!' came a further command, and the beatings continued.

Thutmose, still at the window, appeared somewhat bored at the spectacle. 'Is that all there is? When my father was alive, I saw thousands.'

'There will be more,' promised Hepu. 'Every year we will pay a visit to the towns of Canaan to retrieve what is due to us and punish those who resist, and we'll deport the trouble-makers along with some of the most beautiful women of the land. Do you have any advice as to how we should dispose of them? There have been some serious accidents lately in the gold mines of the Eastern Desert and in the granite quarries. Perhaps some could be assigned there. And we could add more workers to the construction of your memorial temple, which will begin soon.'

It took only a few seconds for Thutmose to respond. 'I don't care what you do with the vermin, get them out of my sight. I have more important business to attend to. However, if there are any winsome girls, you will present them to me later when they are bathed and groomed.'

'All will be done as you wish,' acknowledged the vizier, 'but there is more to show you.' Hepu waved away the prisoners, who promptly arose and were quickly escorted away while several pairs of huge men waddled in holding the handles of extremely heavy baskets. With their beards and wool tunics, they were obviously Canaanites, and after being given orders not to look forward or upward, they emptied their cargo on a long, fine mat placed before them. It was a fortune in assorted gold and jewellery, and the latest haul from the subjugated territories to the east.

'This is good,' acknowledged the pharaoh. 'This pleases me. Melt down the gold and retrieve whatever precious stones are attached. I would like to have a spectacular necklace made for my mother.' The jewellery was quickly replaced in the baskets and their bearers dismissed.

'And now,' announced Hepu, 'here is something very special for his majesty.' Upon a prearranged signal by the vizier to the guards at the entrance, the front doors of the palace opened and dozens of beautifully attended horses pranced in with leather bridles and ostrich plume headdresses. There were several pairs pulling chariots and Thutmose could barely contain his excitement. Leaving Hepu at the window, he uncharacteristically rushed down to the courtyard to admire the magnificent steeds. If there was one thing Thutmose loved, it was horses, and these beauties from the east were stunning.

## PRECIOUS AND SHINY

Most human societies seem to value gold for its relative scarcity, its gleam and lovely colour, and its malleability, allowing it to be used in an infinite number of ways. The ancient Egyptians referred to the metal as 'the flesh of the gods', and silver, even more rare for them, as 'the bones of the gods'. Apart from these cherished materials, gemstones including carnelian, amazonite, lapis lazuli, garnet, amethyst and turquoise were prized for use in the making of sophisticated jewellery. The immense value and quantity of gold prized by the Egyptians can be represented by the contents of the virtually intact tomb of the 18th-dynasty ruler, Tutankhamun. Within were found numerous items covered in gold, and the innermost of his three nesting coffins was made completely of that material, and weighs over 110 kilograms (243 pounds).

The ruler walked among them all, inspecting each individually and complimenting them, before enthusiastically declaring that all were welcome in the royal stables. 'Gold and horses,' he yelled over to Hepu. 'The few decent things to come out of Canaan!'

Having been delegated by Thutmose to pass judgement on the captives, Hepu consulted with the commanders, some of whom had personal knowledge of specific individuals. Some were extremely cooperative, but there were others who had been notable resisters and yet somehow survived the trip to Egypt without being executed. 'Send the worst to the gold mines,' concluded the vizier. 'If the harsh conditions in the desert won't pacify them, their lack of food and water, should they rebel, will likely cause them to comply. And their devious Egyptian criminal co-workers will keep them alert.'

As for most of the others, there was a great demand for one of the most obnoxious tasks in the entire land: the making of mud bricks, which were regularly required by the millions. It involved wallowing in wet muck all day long at the edge of the river, and often in the hot sun depending upon the season. Mud was mixed with scraps of straw foraged from the fields, and then pushed into rectangular moulds before being left to dry in the sun. After that, the bricks were transported where needed via heavy baskets balanced on a pole across the shoulders, or if lucky, on a donkey.

It was a wretched job, but those in the mud pits might find that not only could they communicate in mutually intelligible foreign tongues distinct from that of the

Egyptians, but they might be related or know people in common. No matter where they originated from in the east, they shared one trait: they had all quickly learned a handful of Egyptian words and phrases such as 'kneel', 'bow', 'look down', 'hurry', 'quiet', 'quickly' and 'eat'. Hepu decided that most would be assigned to Thebes, where they could be put to use making bricks for the memorial temple of the current living and ruling pharaoh.

For the captives, the voyage south to Thebes would be no less uncomfortable than that which brought them to Memphis. They would be kept close together on deck throughout the day and night, and any attempt to escape would likely result in drowning. Any disrespect to their guards would provoke a swift and brutal blow or a stab.

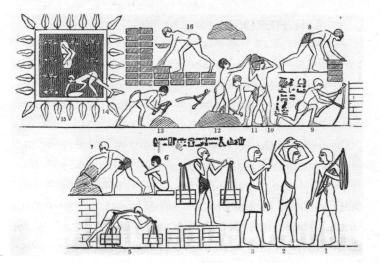

**BRICK-MAKING: ONE OF THE MOST MISERABLE JOBS IN ANCIENT EGYPT**

Once in Thebes, the captives would be kept in crowded barracks where there was little room for anything other than cramped sleeping on mats. They would be fed their bread and beer, but they could expect long days, humiliating insults from their overseers, and the possibility of death from injury or exhaustion.

Not resembling Egyptians, speaking with a strong accent at best, and a lack of knowledge of the Nile's geography, made it nearly impossible to run away without being noticed as a foreigner. The escapee would be returned and harshly punished as an example, and perhaps sent to a job that would make brick-making seem relaxed.

## THE HERDSMAN AND THE POTTER

In Thebes, Senna was about to engage in one of his most favourite pastimes. Every once in a while, when the estate owner was away for a few days, the herdsman would keep the cows in their pen with fodder he had collected for the occasion, instead of bringing them out to graze. With all under control, he would meet his friend Roy the potter for an excursion to one of the local state facilities for the production of bread and beer. With untold thousands dependent upon both products for their payment and sustenance, it was a major enterprise, but not particularly complicated.

With a mutual interest in drinking strong beer and other alcoholic beverages, Roy and Senna had met each other several years previously while attending one of the local festivals. After an evening of frivolity, both drank a bit too much and passed out. The following morning, the two strangers awakened simultaneously next to each other in a vegetable garden whose ownership was unknown. It was a bonding experience and the two had been close friends ever since.

At the bread and brew compound, Senna and Roy were greeted by a mutual acquaintance, Neferhebet, who had an instinct that his two friends would appear on that very day. Neferhebet was a general supervisor for the operation who attempted to make sure that both the quantity and quality of the products were acceptable, if not good. 'Did you bring your own straws?' he asked. Both of the visitors pointed to long, hollow reeds tucked into their loincloths and the tour of the facilities began. 'Let's start with the bakery! Here are the granaries,' Neferhebet pointed out. 'They are rarely empty, thanks to our ruler and the other gods who have blessed us with abundant harvests, and your taxes. We bake bread all day long, every day of the year. It's made from wheat or barley, and every loaf is delicious and beneficial to health.'

Not far away were dozens of women crushing the grain into flour, while others mixed it with water to form pliable dough. Dozens of large conical ovens, curiously similar to those which fired pots, produced bread in several shapes. Some were baked in cone-shaped moulds, and others were left to rise into circular loaves. Hot from the oven, they were profoundly delectable, and certainly edible for a few days to come.

Neferhebet was right. The bread was fresh and sustaining, and it was widely distributed in the region, with other similar facilities doing the same elsewhere in Egypt. On special occasions such as festivals, a little sweetening with honey or dates could make it seem more special and Neferhebet made sure a bit of that was available for his friends. Senna and Roy had no need to ask for samples of such as it was part of the routine, but the next part of the tour was their favourite.

Having sated themselves on freshly baked bread, the next stop was the brewery. Roy especially enjoyed visiting the brewery and looking around the facility. Everywhere were products of his own hands, and in his focused mind, he felt that he could recognize each one. Over the years, he had manufactured untold thousands of beer jars as commissioned by this very brewery, and to him they were his children. Once, he made the mistake of expressing that intimate feeling to Senna, who had cruelly laughed.

Hundreds and hundreds of large jars sat along a wall in the compound. Fresh water from the Nile had been strained and then poured into each pot. Afterwards, a chunk of fresh bread was thrown into each vessel, which would cause fermentation, producing a lightly alcoholic brew after a few days. The beer was strong enough to kill whatever contaminating evils might be present in the ever-complex flowing waters of the Nile, yet weak enough as not to interfere with the efficiency of those working on projects of the state. At its best, the beer would be nutritious, yet have a slightly numbing effect to distract from tedium.

Both Roy and Senna removed their straws, a cue that Neferhebet understood well. It was time to move from the ordinary to the special and sample the beer reserved for grand occasions such as festivals, or daily consumption for those who could afford it. Those involved in its production expected favours in return for sharing the special brew. From Roy, Neferhebet expected customized ceramic vessels to delight his friends and relatives. From Senna, he anticipated random cuts of beef when available.

Neferhebet led his two friends to a large covered room facing away from the busy production area. On a bench off to one side were a couple of well-dressed officials, each smiling blissfully with a jar between his knees and a long straw poised at his mouth. Roy recognized one of them; it was his supervisor from the ceramic kilns, but it was likely that his boss was in no condition to remember the experience, no matter what transpired.

Neferhebet felt Roy's apprehension and assured him that there would be no repercussions, before escorting his visitors to a special jar in the corner. The brewer pried a mud stopper off its top and confidently proclaimed: 'This is the best beer that either of you has ever tasted.' The beer had been concocted with a handful of barley bread, and a subtle balance of dates, honey, coriander and cloves. After a calculated number of days of blending and fermentation, the beer had been strained to filter out the bread slop and other chunks of residue, to produce a smooth and potent libation.

Both Roy and Senna thrust their long straws into the jar and both agreed with the brewer. It was exceptional, and Neferhebet, too, took several big sips. It wasn't long before the three were exceptionally jolly, and Senna proclaimed his love for all in the universe. Meanwhile, Roy's supervisor had collapsed on the floor with a smile on his face, and would likely awaken with no understanding of his surroundings, or even what day it was. Roy was safe!

Not far away, Baki was beginning to harvest his crops, a process that would take several days. The wheat and barley had grown well this year thanks to his months of hard effort, and the farmer recruited several members of his extended family to assist in reaping the crops. First, the ears were cut off near the top of the stalks using wooden sickles outfitted with flint blades. The grain was then gathered up in baskets to be thrown on to a threshing floor next to Baki's home and then trampled by a couple of donkeys. With the husks thus separated, the grain was thrust up in the air with scoops and forks, allowing breezes

**HARVESTING GRAIN WITH SICKLES**

to blow away the chaff. The cereal was then collected and given a first sieving to remove stray straw and rocks, and ultimately deposited in a granary for use all year.

There would be plenty of grain to sustain Baki's family, and much of it would be traded throughout the year for various goods and services, or handed out to pay state taxes. Some of the grain would be shared with the relatives assisting in the harvest, of course, and there were people in the village who were far more interested in the dry, earless stalks remaining in the field. It had plenty of uses including straw for brick-making, fuel for fires, and animal fodder. Some of it would go to Senna, who provided the donkeys. He would use the fodder to feed his herd during his special days away.

## THE NUBIANS

Not long after having received the human and physical tribute from the eastern subjugated territories, Thutmose set sail on his extravagant boat to hold court in his exceptionally opulent palace in Thebes. Temple projects were on his mind, as were displays of goods coming from another region subjugated by Egypt: Nubia. The trip would take several days and he personally preferred to be active on land, rather than having to make the repeated and necessary voyages up and down the Nile, even with such a beautiful and comfortable conveyance as his royal boat.

The arrival at the palace this time, however, was especially welcoming. New furniture had arrived, made of the best wood, ivory and gold, all bearing the names Menkheperure Thutmose, incised or inlaid. The royal workshop had been busy, and the carpenters were told to be at their absolute best. Although there was nothing in Egypt that one might consider a 'forest', there were a good many trees that could be put to use. Acacias and tamarisks were common as was sycamore, but some of the finest timber came from elsewhere. Cedar was especially desirable but had to be imported from hostile lands in the eastern Mediterranean. The logs had to be dragged from the hills to the shore, and then towed behind ships to reach the Nile. The huge royal ships were made out of this fine material, their planks and wooden fittings shaped with copper saws and chisels. And from the south, ebony was cherished, as the ruler was about to find out.

Ptahhotep greeted the ruler effusively, anxious to share a few bits of news of note, which at least this time wasn't much. There was, however, a contingent of Nubians awaiting with a display of tribute to honour the new pharaoh. Similar to the spectacle of Canaanites he had just recently experienced in Memphis, Thutmose had witnessed displays of treasures from the south several times while his father was still alive.

In reality, Thutmose wasn't sure which people he despised the most, the Canaanites and the other eastern peoples, or the Nubians in the south. Gold and horses, though, were always appreciated, and the Nubians were well known for their occasional surprises. After resting and donning a simple headdress, Thutmose took his place on his new throne in the audience hall with a full view of the exterior courtyard, his duo of fan-bearers ready to cool their master. As expected, scribes seated with their legs crossed bowed their heads as did the dozens of soldiers with their daggers and spears. Incense wafted throughout and the scene was set for pageantry and intimidation.

Ptahhotep soon approached to announce the proceedings. 'Your majesty, there are several Nubian chiefs here. They are not captives. They have come to show their respect with their presence and their gifts.'

'Have them approach,' commanded the ruler. The great exterior palace doors opened and a half dozen men approached with feathers protruding from their headbands and colourful skirts wrapped around their waists. Their wide bead collars and golden armlets and nose rings clearly indicated their wealth and importance. The chiefs knew exactly what to do and fell on to their knees, until prompted by the vizier to arise.

**NUBIANS PRESENT TRIBUTE INCLUDING GOLD AND A GIRAFFE**

Ptahhotep faced Thutmose and explained their purpose. 'The chiefs wish to celebrate the new king with hopes that Egypt's relationship with the lands to the south will be peaceful rather than warlike.'

'What did they bring for us?' asked the ruler impatiently. The vizier waved at the chiefs and after a few shouts in their own language, an amazing parade of perhaps fifty dark-skinned foreign porters entered the courtyard, with each one leaving the items they were carrying displayed in front of the pharaoh, before turning to return with more items. As instructed, their eyes were not to meet those of the ruler unless ordered otherwise.

The first porters brought in dozens of heavy chunks of the highly desirable ebony wood, which they stacked off to the side. Next came a line of about forty men, each with an elephant tusk balanced over a shoulder to be formed into a pile. The royal craftsmen would certainly appreciate that; the ivory from the tusks was much preferred to that derived from hippo teeth. Next came dozens of cheetah skins, no doubt obtained at great risk, and a large number of baskets containing incense.

Several in attendance were startled when a loud rhythmic banging began. Four Nubian men stepped forth pounding on drums covered in leopard skin, while half a dozen young women wearing nothing more than ankle bracelets began whirling and skipping to the tempo. The performance was short and Ptahhotep seemed particularly impressed. 'I'll find nice places for them in the household,' he promised.

As expected, at some point there would be exotic animals, and the Nubian chiefs did not disappoint in this regard. Several pairs of ostriches pranced in, each on a separate leash, their heads darting every which way to take in the strange sights before them. The birds were valued for their massive feathers and their huge eggs, and when they died, their meat would no doubt be a rare treat. A baby elephant and a small giraffe came next, and although Thutmose found such creatures slightly amusing when he was much younger, as a young adult he concluded that they were impractical and not of much use. His grandfather

## NUBIA

The land of Nubia extended south from ancient Egypt's southern border near the modern city of Aswan to about where the city of Khartoum is situated in modern Sudan, and was home to many tribes and several sophisticated civilizations. Due to Egypt's desire to control its southern border and also obtain rare or valuable goods and raw materials, its relationship with the peoples of that region was often contentious. Following the New Kingdom, during the time period Egyptologists refer to as the 'Third Intermediate Period', Egypt was ruled by conquering Nubian kings for about ninety years. Although receiving much less attention from scholars than Egypt, ancient Nubia has increasingly become a focus for archaeological study, and 'Nubiology' its own speciality.

Thutmose III actually had his own zoo, but all of those animals were long dead, and the new ruler had other interests.

Although the pharaoh was surprisingly impressed with the gifts, he leaned over to Ptahhotep to ask him a pressing question: 'Where's the gold?' The answer came immediately when several large baskets of the metal, much of it in flakes and nuggets, were carried in and prominently displayed. Thutmose stood up with a smile on his face. 'Ptahhotep. Let the chiefs know that I thank them for their gifts, and they are welcome to visit us with more. We expect that they and their people will respect our dominance of their land, and that when they encounter any Egyptians in Nubia, they will treat them with kindness as we have treated them here today.' Ptahhotep conveyed the message to a translator who addressed the chiefs, who once again took to their knees as Thutmose left the room.

# Fourth Month of the
# Season of Harvest

## THE TAX ASSESSOR, THE
## ACCOUNTANT AND A CORONATION

The palace at Memphis was bustling with activity. With the official coronation taking place in just a month on the occasion of the New Year, there were innumerable details to be addressed, not only at Memphis, but at several other major locations. It was far more complicated than a royal funeral but a proper coronation was utterly essential to formalize Thutmose's role as both a king and a god. Like a royal funeral, such ceremonies rarely took place, but there were surviving descriptions, and even some older advisors who could instruct.

The coronation would begin at Memphis, where Thutmose would be entrusted with symbols as presented by priests representing various gods. The Red Crown symbolizing Lower Egypt would be placed upon the ruler's head to be worn simultaneously with the White Crown representing Upper Egypt, emphasizing his sovereignty over both regions. There was a Blue Crown denoting his role as commander of the military, and a headdress bearing the cobra and vulture goddesses would also emphasize the pharaoh as the Lord of the Two Lands. The ceremony would be elaborate, and even though Thutmose had already announced his titles at the death of his father, they would be regularly proclaimed as reinforcement. It wouldn't be long before the Egyptian world could breathe a second sigh of relief, as they would have not only a new ruler, but one consecrated by the gods.

Down in Thebes, Baki scanned his harvested field with a sense of pride. Months of work had resulted in a substantial amount of grain that would serve him well through the year. Soon the Nile would rise again, and the annual cycle would be in force again, provided *maat* had been well maintained by Thutmose, and the sun continued to rise. There was one aspect of the yearly routine that Baki despised, and it arrived in familiar form, coming down the village road and stopping at each farmer's house in turn. It was the taxman sent from the government to assess the bounty of fields not owned by the state, and then calculate a payment.

Many of the farmers completely resented the process. A portion of their hard work was being taken for which they saw little in return. Much of it went to pay other workers and bureaucrats who were employed on government projects such as temples, palaces and huge monuments glorifying the ruler. Baki accepted that there was not much he could do about it, and unlike his attempt earlier in the year to hide from his 'volunteer' labour, he met the scribe at the door, prepared to hear of the fate of his efforts.

The well-dressed accountant was accompanied by a large armed soldier, who appeared rather bored by his assignment and stood quietly by as the scribe consulted a sheet of papyrus paper before sitting down on the brick bench in front of the farmer's house. 'I assume that your boundaries are the same as they were last year?' the accountant enquired. Baki was tempted to claim that a portion of his fields had been washed away during the flooding earlier in the year, but quickly dismissed the idea: such falsifications were not taken lightly.

Making some calculations in his head, the accountant wrote down a number and announced his assessment. 'There will be ten more large baskets of wheat than last year. With our new ruler, Menkheperure Thutmose, may he live, thrive and be healthy, there are many new adjustments and projects.' Baki knew it was futile to complain. He would begrudgingly deliver the grain at the appointed time and place and put it out of his mind, and Egypt's massive storage granaries would once again be full.

## A Wedding in the Village

A couple of weeks later there was excitement in the village. A simple fisherman and a young widowed weaver were to be wed. There wasn't a lot of formality to it. Weni and Tameret had both agreed to the arrangement and the two would move into her house. Her sister, Satmut, would need to tolerate their presence until she, too, found a mate. The wedding feast was typically noisy, chaotic and fun and the food was exceptional as expected. Senna the herdsman had somehow 'acquired' a choice leg from what had been a 'severely injured' bull, and strong beer was provided by friends at the brewery.

Tameret was dressed beautifully in a bright white pleated linen dress, courtesy of the ladies at her workplace, and Weni was outfitted in the cleanest kilt he had ever worn. His fellow fishermen made him scrub down in the river over and over again until no scent of carp remained, at least for the big party. Songs were joyously sung to the accompaniment of drums, rattles and flutes, and the dancing girls gyrated through, and around, the crowd. Off in a corner, the groom's best friend, Nefer, was having a lively chat with Satmut, who seemed to be smiling and blushing. Their conversation lasted hours.

Off in the distance a man could be seen approaching the village with a donkey in tow as darkness began to fall. It soon became clear that it was Dagi, the young palace scribe, coming to pay a special visit, clearly comfortable this time, and without hesitation. All parted as Dagi approached the new couple and removed a couple of large containers hanging in nets from the donkey's sides. 'Two jars of the finest imported wine from Canaan for your special celebration!' he announced. Roy the potter stood to the side giggling as he recognized one of the imitation Canaanite jugs, and the party continued until the first glow in the east indicated that Re once again had been reborn.

# Epilogue

The reign of Thutmose IV remains somewhat mysterious to Egyptologists, who at one time considered him to be an obscure transitional historical figure between the time of warrior pharaohs such as his grandfather and father, Thutmose III and Amenhotep II, and his son Amenhotep III, who presided over a period of incredible wealth and relative peace. He reigned for about ten years (*c.* 1400–1390 BC), engaged in few major military conquests, had several wives and children, and held his mother, Tiaa, in especially high regard. One of his wives was a princess contributed by a king of Mitanni, a Syrian rival of Egypt, and an example of international diplomacy that would be repeated by future kings.

We do not know the cause of his death, although his mummy has been described as 'extremely emaciated', suggesting, perhaps, that he might have died of disease. Like his father, Thutmose was buried in the tomb he commissioned in the Great Place, known today as the Valley of the Kings. Tiaa likely outlived her son.

What remains especially intriguing about the reign of Thutmose IV is what appears to be some sort of controversy around his obtaining the throne. The giant 'Dream Stele' between the paws of the Sphinx continues to serve as the major source of speculation for such; the story about the sun god contacting Prince Thutmose possibly being a legitimization story preserved in stone for the ages. As noted in the introduction to this book, the scenario presented here, that is, that Amenhotep II preferred a son other than Thutmose to be his successor, is purely speculative on the part of this author, but, nonetheless, plausible; likewise, the storyline that he was a very special favourite of his mother.

The surviving monuments of Thutmose IV aren't extensive, perhaps due to the short length of his reign. Among other projects at various sites in Egypt, he made additions to the great temple of Karnak at Thebes, although most there were dismantled and their stones reused by later rulers. Impressively, he raised a huge obelisk there that had been initiated by his grandfather. At the time this was the largest such monument ever erected. (It now stands in Rome where it was transported from Egypt in the fourth century AD.) A few stone statues of Thutmose IV remain, one of the most prominent depicting the ruler seated with his mother, to whom he granted special titles including 'God's Wife of Amun', the highest level of priestess at that time.

Thutmose's successor, Amenhotep III, reigned for thirty-eight years and utilized Egypt's wealth to the maximum with the construction of spectacular monuments, both religious and personal, including luxurious palaces for his own use. Amenhotep III enhanced the temples to Amun at

Thebes, an indicator of the continuing primacy of the god. What survives today of the ruler's own memorial temple shows that it was massive and impressive like few others.

His son Amenhotep IV shook Egypt's status quo when he embarked on a fixation with a manifestation of the sun known as the Aten, the sun represented as a fiery disk with its nurturing rays. He changed his name to 'Akhenaten' – 'Beneficial to the Sun-Disk' – and built his own political capital far away from the political and religious centres of Memphis and Thebes. With its emphasis on the Aten, Akhenaten's cult was borderline monotheistic, and essentially denigrated the other gods with their temples and priests, including the powerful and wealthy cult of Amun. Some scholars have argued that the emergence of the Aten as a substantial deity grew under the reign of Thutmose IV and then his successor, but regardless, the seventeen years or so of Akhenaten's rule are a fascinating period in Egyptian history involving not only religious innovations, but artistic ones as well.

The death of Akhenaten certainly brought relief to the many that he shunned, and after one or two ephemeral short-lived successors, the modernly famous 'boy-king' Tutankhaten (meaning 'Living Image of the Sun-Disk'), became ruler, with a restoration to the old order symbolized by a change of his name to 'Tutankhamun' (Living Image of Amun). Until the discovery of his virtually intact tomb in 1922, he, like Thutmose IV, was considered an obscure transitional figure, in his case, between the bizarre Akhenaten interlude and the restoration of strong pharaohs. After Tutankhamun's brief reign of about a decade, his successor was a priest followed by a military general, and with Rameses I, another dynasty, the 19th, began.

The 19th dynasty brought about new rounds of foreign conflicts, and warrior pharaohs. One of the most prominent, Rameses II, ruled for over six decades and, like Amenhotep III, was a prolific builder of monuments including numerous celebrating himself. Some might argue that another fighting pharaoh, Rameses III of the 20th dynasty, was the last great pharaoh of the era as he successfully repelled attacks by invaders from the sea and elsewhere. The end of the 20th dynasty is considered the end of the New Kingdom, and some would argue also the end of Egypt's true greatness. With economic stress and political confusion, most of the already-robbed tombs in the Valley of the Kings were dismantled. The majority of the royal mummies interred there had been ravaged by thieves, but pious priests rewrapped the bodies and hid them elsewhere. More on that below.

The history of Egypt following the New Kingdom is incredibly complicated. There were at various times episodes of foreign domination in Egypt from such places as Libya, Nubia, Assyria and Persia, along with the Greeks and the Romans. After Egypt was conquered by Alexander the Great in the fourth century BC, Greeks ruled the land for about three hundred years. Greek colonists introduced their language, religion and culture, which highly influenced Egyptian civilization. The early introduction of Christianity to Egypt, too, had an effect, and later the religion of Islam – accompanied by the Arabic language and culture – would dominate as it continues to do today. The result is that much of the ancient Egyptian culture with its pharaohs, gods and hieroglyphs seemingly 'vanished', to be rediscovered by those who found it of interest many centuries later.

## CONTROLLING THE NILE

The construction of the massive 'Aswan High Dam' in southern Egypt in the 1960s has been a mixed blessing. With a giant reservoir, 'Lake Nasser', formed behind the structure, Egypt has little fear of flooding or drought downstream, and now several crops and harvests are possible each year. The dam also produces a great quantity of electricity. However, without the natural flooding and the annual natural renewal of the soil, artificial fertilizers are now required as a substitute and can have a negative effect in the long run. The creation of the dam also instigated a cultural emergency when Lake Nasser threatened to drown numerous archaeological sites. International rescue efforts documented many sites as the waters rose, and entire temples were saved by dismantling them and moving them to higher ground nearby or elsewhere. One of these temples, from the site of Dendur, was given as a gift from Egypt to the United States for its assistance in the salvage of the monuments, and today can be found re-erected in an atrium at the Metropolitan Museum of Art in New York City.

Despite the historical and cultural changes and transformations, some aspects of the age-old lifestyle continue in modern Egypt similar to that of ancient times. Much of Egypt remains rural and farmers still toil at their crops on the lands along the Nile, although the modern dam built far to the south in Aswan has controlled the annual flooding, and other crops such as sugar cane are now grown. Village homes are often small and made of mud brick, and cows and beasts of burden ply the dusty paths, while fishermen in small boats continue to throw their nets in the river.

## Archaeological Discoveries

Although there were sporadic visits to Egypt by Europeans and other outsiders who were perplexed by its antiquities, most historians see Napoleon's invasion in 1798 as the birth of modern Egyptology. Along with his army he brought along a cadre of artists and scholars to document all things Egyptian, including the remains of its past. Despite being routed by the British three years later, the French published their findings and inspired a great deal of interest in the land of the pharaohs. Among their discoveries was a large stone tablet written in Greek and two Egyptian scripts. The 'Rosetta Stone', as it became known, provided a key to understanding the long-forgotten ancient language and script. After intense study, a Frenchman, Jean-François Champollion, declared its decipherment in 1822. After this breakthrough, the mysterious hieroglyphs could begin to be read, and the study of surviving texts contribute mightily to our knowledge of ancient Egypt.

Expeditions to document Egypt's monuments and collect many of its artefacts first became common in the nineteenth century and, as a result, we have learned what we know about the likes of Amenhotep II and Thutmose IV and their time. Archaeological excavation and documentation techniques evolved significantly during the last couple of centuries, and a few discoveries related to the stories in this book are both significant and interesting.

It was noted above that at the end of the New Kingdom, the rewrapped royal mummies from the Valley of the Kings were hidden. One such cache was found by local tomb robbers on the west bank of Thebes around 1872. Eventually, its existence was brought to the attention of the Egyptian antiquities authorities, who were astonished to find that it was a reused tomb containing over fifty mummies, including many royal individuals from the New Kingdom. A second cache was found in the tomb of Amenhotep II in the Valley of the Kings, which had been robbed in antiquity, but was then used to store twelve mummies, including Thutmose IV, in addition to Amenhotep himself, as one might expect, and the likely remains of one of his sons, probably Webensenu.

Amenhotep II's tomb was discovered in 1898 by the French Egyptologist Victor Loret and apart from the additional mummies and a huge quantity of smashed and intact funerary objects, the ruler himself remained beautifully wrapped in his sarcophagus with a dried bouquet laid atop. The wrappings, though, were not his original, nor was his coffin, which belonged to a later date, but he is one of two royal mummies found in its own tomb. (Tutankhamun is the other exception.)

Most of the royal mummies discovered in the two caches were shipped to the Egyptian Museum in Cairo, where for many years they were available for viewing, off and on, to the public. At one point they were placed in high-tech nitrogen-filled display cases in a more dignified atmosphere. In 2021, most were relocated by way of a spectacular grand parade to the National Museum of Egyptian Civilization, also located in Cairo.

In 1898, Loret found another tomb in the Valley. It was unfinished, undecorated, and in poor condition, and not much was found within. Beginning in the year 2000, a Swiss expedition investigated the tomb and discovered evidence that it belonged to Tiaa, the wife of Amenhotep II and the mother of Thutmose IV, who had been granted the great privilege of being interred there, despite its incomplete state.

During the twentieth century, archaeological excavations continued in the Valley of the Kings and in 1903, Howard Carter discovered the tomb of Thutmose IV while working for an American excavator, Theodore Davis. As was usually the case, the tomb had been ruthlessly robbed. As in the tomb of Amenhotep II, shattered burial goods had been strewn about, probably for the second time. Some prominent ancient graffiti in one of the chambers indicates that the tomb had been first robbed about seventy years after Thutmose's burial and then put back in order. It was, like the other royal tombs, later dismantled as the New Kingdom faded, and the ruler's mummy relocated to a cache as noted above.

## TOMB ROBBERS

Most tomb robbers seem to have been interested in expensive recyclables such as linen, oils, precious metals, gems and jewellery. Gold could be scraped off gilded wooden surfaces and melted down for reuse, the oil transferred to less conspicuous containers, and name tags cut off royal linen. Tomb robbery in ancient Egypt was profitable, but an extremely punishable offence. Some papyrus documents survive that actually record the trials of suspects accused of entering and robbing royal tombs. If convicted, the culprits could be painfully put to death by burning or being impaled on a stake. With an increase of foreign interest in Egypt during the last couple of centuries, tomb robbers were kept busy providing museums and tourists with interesting items for sale. The sale of antiquities in Egypt is now illegal, with severe penalties for engaging in such activities.

In 1906, the Davis expedition discovered the simple undecorated tomb of Amenhotep II's vizier, Amenemopet. Its small rectangular burial chamber was found robbed, with Amenemopet's mummy stripped of its wrappings and lying on the floor among bits and pieces of grave goods. The tomb was covered over during subsequent excavations in the vicinity and its exact location was lost until an American Egyptologist, Kent Weeks, rediscovered the top of its shaft in 1986 by using 'remote sensing' equipment. Beginning in 2008, the author of this book re-excavated the tomb and found more remains of the original burial. The mummy, however, was missing and its location is still unknown. His tomb chapel in the nobles' cemetery has been studied and although bearing painted decoration, it was never completely finished.

A PORTION OF THE VALLEY OF THE KINGS TODAY.
1: THE ENTRANCE OF THE ROYAL TOMB OF AMENHOTEP II. 2: THE
TOMB OF HIS VIZIER, AMENEMOPET. 3: THE SITE WHERE THREE
SMALL TOMBS WERE FOUND CONTAINING THE MUMMIES OF ANIMALS
WHICH WERE PERHAPS THE PETS OF AMENHOTEP

After a decade of work and many impressive discoveries, Theodore Davis proclaimed in 1912 that there was nothing left to discover in the Valley of the Kings. The uncovering of the virtually intact tomb of Tutankhamun ten years later proved otherwise. Today it remains the archaeological discovery to which all other spectacular discoveries are compared. The exploration of Egypt's past continues to this day, with investigations of ancient sites and monuments dating from prehistoric times through the eras of the Greeks and Romans, and beyond. Although few tombs have been found in the Valley of the Kings since Tut's in 1922, research still continues there with efforts to study and conserve the tombs of the pharaohs, and reassess some of the smaller undecorated tombs belonging to officials and lesser royalty scattered in the vicinity.

## Egypt Today

Tourism is an important part of the Egyptian economy and in some years the country has hosted over 10 million visitors. It's a welcoming place; the landscape is generally gorgeous; and there is an amazing amount of interesting and fun things to do. The antiquities, of course, are a huge attraction. One can, for example, visit the famous Old Kingdom pyramids of Giza, and see the Great Sphinx with the 'Dream Stele'. Just south there's not much to see of what was once the capital city of Memphis but the massive ancient cemetery nearby includes pyramids and decorated tombs spanning many ages.

## TOMB OF THE BOY-KING

Despite his relatively minor role in Egyptian history, Tutankhamun is perhaps the most recognizable pharaoh to the modern public. Although there are indications that his royal tomb in the Valley of the Kings was, perhaps, lightly robbed twice, little seems to have been taken and the overwhelming majority of its spectacular contents remained intact and well preserved. Tutankhamun's tomb continues to be a sensation even a century after its discovery, and its contents offer tantalizing clues as to what other royal tombs may have once contained. Its survival is probably due to it being deeply buried under construction rubble from a later tomb built above, and/or from the debris of a desert flash flood. It's fortuitous, too, that the tomb was found in 1922 rather than any time earlier as competent experts were available to document and preserve the thousands of objects found within.

There are numerous fascinating sites all along the Nile before one reaches the city of Luxor, the site of ancient Thebes. On the east bank of the river are found the enormous and complicated Luxor and Karnak temples, with additions to each spanning many centuries. And as of 2021, one can walk between the two with the recently restored ancient processional road.

On the west bank of the Nile, there is likewise plenty to see, and the decorated tombs of officials are popular, including those of the vizier Rekhmire, with its depictions of arts and crafts, and that of Sennefer, with its painted ceiling resembling a grape arbour. There is little to see of the New Kingdom memorial temples of Amenhotep II and Thutmose IV, but a few remain that belonged to others that are truly impressive, especially those of Hatshepsut, Amenhotep III, Seti I, Rameses II and Rameses III.

And there is, of course, the ancient royal New Kingdom cemetery, the Valley of the Kings. Even when busy with tourists, one can be impressed by its tall cliffs, and the pyramid-shaped peak presiding over all. There are about five dozen tombs in the Valley and a few of the more impressive can be visited, although they are open only on a rotating basis. The remarkable tombs of both Amenhotep II and Thutmose IV have both been prepared for visitors and are occasionally accessible. There is also, of course, the incredibly small tomb of Tutankhamun, which for no other reason than its fame is often of high priority for many a tourist.

Tucked against the cliffs not too far away are the remains of the village that housed the workmen who built the tombs in the Valley of the Kings. Archaeologists over the years have exposed the houses of this once-busy settlement and visitors can walk among the ruins and imagine how it must have been in its heyday. Some of its residents had their own small tombs there and a few that are beautifully decorated are available to examine. The foreman of workmen for the Valley of the Kings during the time of Amenhotep II and

Thutmose IV, Kha, accompanied by his wife, Merit, has a tomb here and it was discovered intact in 1906 by an Italian expedition. An unviolated tomb of this sort is a rare find and most of its spectacular contents are displayed in the Egyptian Museum in Torino, Italy.

There are many other sites in the Luxor area worth seeing including another New Kingdom royal cemetery, the so-called Valley of the Queens, and a magnificent museum in the city of Luxor, with a stunning sample of discoveries from ancient Thebes. There are numerous spectacular sites to the south, and all the way to the Mediterranean coast in the north. In short, Egypt is one big, fascinating archaeological site, bursting with prehistoric, pharaonic,

THE MASSIVE RUINS OF THE SPRAWLING TEMPLE OF KARNAK
AT LUXOR, THE SITE OF ANCIENT THEBES

Greek, Roman, Christian and Islamic history, along with an energetic modern culture. There are wonderful museums throughout the country, including the enormous Grand Egyptian Museum outside Cairo near the Giza pyramids.

Outside of Egypt, collections of Egyptian antiquities can be found around the world, the most prominent being in the British Museum (London, UK), the Louvre (Paris, France), the Egyptian Museum (Turin, Italy) and the Metropolitan Museum of Art (New York, USA). Most of the artefacts found in these collections were obtained during times when it was legal to export such items. Today, antiquities are not allowed to leave Egypt, but the country periodically organizes spectacular travelling artefact exhibitions that have attracted millions outside its borders.

Egyptology today remains a vibrant international enterprise. Although the majority of archaeological work in Egypt was once conducted by foreign expeditions, the number of Egyptian projects is quickly catching up and they are regularly making extraordinary discoveries throughout the country. Egyptological societies around the world support the interest of a growing number of enthusiasts at all levels, from the casually curious to the professional, and books, films and websites feed a wide fascination. There are a vast number of questions to answer, and riddles to be solved, and ancient Egypt will likely forever inspire us with a rich sense of wonder.

# Acknowledgements

Appreciation is extended to my very good friend, the late Barbara Mertz (aka Elizabeth Peters/Barbara Michaels), who epitomized the ability to write engagingly on subjects of the past for a general audience. Sherry Ryan, Samuel Ryan and Lois Schwartz are always supportive, and Sherry's editorial comments were invaluable. The editors at Michael O'Mara Books, including Gabriella Nemeth, were helpful and patient. Very special thanks are extended to my excellent friends, Dr Edmund Meltzer and Dr Kenneth Griffin, two brilliant Egyptologists who shared valuable insights and resources.

# Picture Credits

Page 9: Map of 15th century Egypt: David Woodroffe

Page 23: Egyptian deities: E. A. W. Budge, *The Gods of the Egyptians*, 1904

Page 41: Amenhotep II: Denis Forbes / KMT Communications

Page 44: Hieroglyphic name: Donald P. Ryan; Scarab Inscribed with the Throne Name of Amenhotep II: Gift of J. Pierpoint Morgan, 1905 / Metropolitan Museum of Art, New York

Page 46: Relief of Amenhotep II, Luxor Museum / © Meretseger Books, www.meretsegerbooks.com

Page 55: Barque of Amun: Adolf Erman, *Life in Ancient Egypt*, 1904

Page 65: Fishermen: Nina de Garis Davies, *Ancient Egyptian Paintings*, 1936

Page 76: The Great Pyramid and the Great Sphinx: *Description de L'Égypte, c.* 1821

Page 84: Papyrus workers: Norman de Garis Davies, *The Tomb of Puyemre* at Thebes, 1922

Page 87: Wine-makers: Norman de Garis Davies, *The Tomb of Nakht at Thebes*, 1917

Page 88: Canaanite jar: Gift of Bess Myerson, 2001 / Metropolitan Museum of Art, New York

Page 92: Musicians: Norman de Garis Davies, *The Tomb of Nakht at Thebes*, 1917

Page 99: Soldiers: C. R. Lepsius, *Denkmaeler aus Aegypten und Aethiopien*, 1900

Page 108: Funeral: E. A. W. Budge, *The Book of the Dead* (Papyrus of Hunefer), 1899

Page 117: Medical text: Cyril P. Bryan, *The Papyrus Ebers*, 1930 / Wellcome Collection (CC BY 4.0)

Page 127: Giza tomb: Georg Steindorff, *Zeitschrift für Ägyptishe Sprache und Altertumskunde*, 1927

Page 133: Ploughing: Norman de Garis Davies, *The Tomb of Nakht at Thebes*, 1917

Page 148: Village ruins: Denis Whitfill

Page 151: Tomb plan of Amenhotep II: Victor Loret, Bulletin de l'Institut d'Égypte, Cairo 9, 1899

Page 153: The Viceroy's Boat, Tomb of Huy: Facsimile painting by Charles K. Wilkinson, *c.* 1926-1927 / Rogers Fund, 1930 / Metropolitan Museum of Art, New York

Page 157: Sculpture of Thutmose IV: Denis Forbes / KMT Communications

Page 160: Hieroglyphic titles: Donald P. Ryan; Cartouche of King Thutmose IV: Magica / Alamy

Page 165: Weavers, Tomb of Khnumhotep: Facsimile painting by Norman de Garis Davies / Rogers Fund, 1933 / Metropolitan Museum of Art, New York

Page 169: Fowling: Norman de Garis Davies, *The Tomb of Nakht at Thebes*, 1917

Page 178: Canopic Jars: Gift of Henry H. Getty, Charles L. Hutchinson, and Norman W. Harris / Art Institute of Chicago

Page 181: Book of the Dead: E. A. W. Budge, *The Book of the Dead* (Papyrus of Ani), 1894

Page 185: Workshop: Norman de Garis Davies, *The Tomb of Two Sculptors at Thebes*, 1914

Page 193: Royal tomb pillar: Giulio Farina, *La Pittura Egiziana*, 1929

Page 202: The Great Sphinx and the 'Dream Stele': Denis Forbes / KMT Communications

Page 220: Brick-making: William C. Prime, *Boat Life in Egypt and Nubia*, 1857; facsimile illustration based on depictions in the Tomb of Rekh-Mi-Re at Thebes

Page 225: Harvesting: Norman de Garis Davies, *The Tomb of Nakht at Thebes*, 1917

Page 228: Nubians: Norman and Nina de Garis Davies, *The Tomb of Huy*, 1926

Page 248: Valley of the Kings: Donald P. Ryan

Page 252: Great Hypostyle Hall, Temple of Karnak: Whatafoto / Shutterstock.com

# Bibliography

Morris Bierbrier, *The Tomb-Builders of the Pharaohs*, 1993

James Henry Breasted, *Ancient Records of Egypt*, 1907

Betsy M. Bryan, *The Reign of Thutmose IV*, 1991

Peter Der Manuelian, *Studies in the Reign of Amennophis II*, 1987

Aidan Dodson and Dyan Hilton, *The Complete Royal Families of Ancient Egypt*, 2004

Dennis C. Forbes, *Imperial Lives: Illustrated Biographies of Significant New Kingdom Egyptians*, 2005

Carolyn Graves-Brown, *Dancing for Hathor*, 2010

Rosalind Hall, *Egyptian Textiles*, 1986

Colin Hope, *Egyptian Pottery*, 1987

Patrick Houlihan, *The Animal World of the Pharaohs*, 1997

Salima Ikram and Aidan Dodson, *The Mummy in Ancient Egypt*, 1998

Salima Ikram and Aidan Dodson, *The Tomb in Ancient Egypt*, 2008

Rosalind and Jac. Janssen, *Growing Up and Getting Old in Ancient Egypt*, 2007

Miriam Lichtheim, *Ancient Egyptian Literature*, 2006

Lise Manniche, *City of the Dead*, 1987

Lise Manniche, *Music and Musicians in Ancient Egypt*, 1991

John Nunn, *Ancient Egyptian Medicine*, 1996

William H. Peck, *The Material World of Ancient Egypt*, 2013

Donald Redford, ed., *The Oxford Encyclopedia of Ancient Egypt*, 2001

Nicholas Reeves and Richard Wilkinson, *The Complete Valley of the Kings*, 1996

Serge Sauneron, *The Priests of Ancient Egypt*, 2000

Garry J. Shaw, *The Pharaoh: Life at Court and on Campaign*, 2012

Ian Shaw, ed., *The Oxford History of Ancient Egypt*, 2000

W. K. Simpson et al., eds., *The Literature of Ancient Egypt: An Anthology of Stories, Instructions, and Poetry*, 2003

John Taylor, *Death and the Afterlife in Ancient Egypt*, 2001

Joyce Tyldesley, *Daughters of Isis: Women of Ancient Egypt*, 1995

Joyce Tyldesley, *The Complete Queens of Egypt*, 2006

Richard H. Wilkinson, *The Complete Temples of Ancient Egypt*, 2000

Hilary Wilson, *Egyptian Food and Drink*, 1988

## Recommended further reading

Peter Clayton, *Chronicle of the Pharaohs*, 2006

Aidan Dodson, *Monarchs of the Nile*, 2016

Dennis C. Forbes, *Tombs. Treasures. Mummies. Seven Great Discoveries of Egyptian Archaeology*, 1998

T. G. H. James, *Pharaoh's People*, 1994

Mark Lehner, *The Complete Pyramids*, 1997

Bill Manley, *Egyptian Hieroglyphs for Complete Beginners*, 2012

Barbara Mertz, *Temples, Tombs and Hieroglyphs: A Popular History of Ancient Egypt*, 2007

Barbara Mertz, *Red Land, Black Land: Daily Life in Ancient Egypt*, 2008

Nicholas Reeves, *Ancient Egypt: The Great Discoveries*, 2000

Donald P. Ryan, *Ancient Egypt on Five Deben a Day*, 2010

Donald P. Ryan, *Beneath the Sands of Egypt: Adventures of an Unconventional Archaeologist*, 2010

Donald P. Ryan, *24 Hours in Ancient Egypt*, 2018

A. J. Spencer, *The British Museum Book of Ancient Egypt*, 2007

Nigel and Helen Strudwick, *Thebes in Egypt: A Guide to the Tombs and Temples of Ancient Luxor*, 1999

Joyce Tyldesley, *The Penguin Book of Myths and Legends of Ancient Egypt*, 2012

Richard H. Wilkinson, *The Complete Gods and Goddesses of Ancient Egypt*, 2003

Richard H. Wilkinson, *Reading Egyptian Art*, 1994

Richard H. Wilkinson, *Symbol and Magic in Egyptian Art* 1999

Toby Wilkinson, *Lives of the Ancient Egyptians: Pharaohs, Queens, Courtiers and Commoners*, 2007

# Index

Entries for illustrative material are shown in *italics*.

### N

### O

### P